Living on the Edge

our personal Antarctic story

by Yvonne Claypole

HarperCollins*Publishers*

Every effort has been made by the author to contact the copyright holders
of selected quoted material contained herein. Any copyright holder who
may have been inadvertently overlooked is welcome to contact the publisher.

HarperCollins*Publishers*

First published in Australia in 2001
Reprinted in 2001
by HarperCollins*Publishers* Pty Limited
ABN 36 009 913 517
A member of the HarperCollins*Publishers* (Australia) Pty Limited Group
www.harpercollins.com.au

HarperCollins*Publishers*
25 Ryde Road, Pymble, Sydney, NSW 2073, Australia
31 View Road, Glenfield, Auckland 10, New Zealand
77–85 Fulham Palace Road, London, W6 8JB, United Kingdom
Hazelton Lanes, 55 Avenue Road, Suite 2900, Toronto, Ontario M5R 3L2
and 1995 Markham Road, Scarborough, Ontario M1B 5M8, Canada
10 East 53rd Street, New York NY 10022, USA

National Library of Australia Cataloguing-in-Publication data:

Claypole, Yvonne.
    Living on the edge: a personal Antarctic story.
    ISBN 0 7322 6915 6.
    1. Claypole, Yvonne. 2. Claypole, Jim. 3. Antarctica –
    Description and travel. I. Title.
919.89

Cover photography by Lindsay Kelley
Map: The Telltale Art — Trudi Canavan
Cover and internal design by Melanie Calabretta, HarperCollins Design Studio
Typeset in 11/18 Ocean Sans MT by HarperCollins Design Studio
Printed and bound in Australia by Griffin Press on 79gsm Bulky Paperback White

7 6 5 4 3 2   01 02 03 04

For Jim

Contents

Acknowledgements

The achievement of my dream was only possible through the encouragement and support of a huge number of people.

My heartfelt thanks to our family and friends, sponsors, colleagues and virtual strangers who were swept up on our wonderful adventure and shared the journey with us. Without you, Expedition Antarctica wouldn't have become a reality.

Jim and I are particularly grateful to the following sponsors and individuals:

New Idea,

NSA Australia Pty Ltd (Juice Plus),

Telstra,

Nine Network Australia Pty Ltd,

Also: Amcor Ltd, Australian Antarctic Division, Vicky Battin, Bogong Equipment, Bollè, John Dunn, Email Training Services P/L, Freedom Foods, HJ Heinz Australia P/L, Vaughn Greenhill, Rhonda Juniper, Kingtread P/L, Linda Lancaster, L'Oreal, Don and Margie McIntyre, MacPac Wilderness Equipment P/L, Alan and Jan Parker, John Roth, Superior Quilt Company – Seaford, Department of

Education Victoria – Curriculum Development and Learning Technologies Section, Steve Williams, the Tokarczyk Family, York Optical Company P/L.

To the clubs, companies and individuals who donated funds on our behalf to the Breast Cancer Network-Australia, thank you.

YVONNE CLAYPOLE

Prologue

I went to the woods because I wished to live
deliberately, to front any essential facts of life,
and see if I could not learn what I had to teach,
and not, when I came to die to discover
that I had not lived.

H.D. Thoreau

I was cold and wet and lay crumpled in a heap like a rag doll dumped in the rain by a thoughtless child. The noises in my head seemed far away and somehow not important. I let the darkness wash over me again and closed my eyes.

I thought I heard Jim call my name. Struggling to focus, I could see he was standing near the companionway peering down at me anxiously. His hair was plastered against his head, his wet clothing hung heavily from his body and blood streaked his face.

The yacht was pitching and bucking wildly while being hammered by huge waves. The screaming of the wind through the rigging and the water washing over the cabin made it near impossible to hear what Jim was saying. Clearly a storm of horrific magnitude had blown up around us and *Spirit of Sydney* was battling massive seas.

'Yvonne! Yvonne!'

I tried to focus on Jim's shape before me. I was disorientated and had no idea that I was slumped in the skipper's bunk on the opposite side of the cabin, or that I was sharing it with an assortment of items that had flown out of lockers and landed around me. The large fire extinguisher that normally hung on the wall nearby was jammed between the head of the bunk and my head. If I had looked closely I would have seen bits of skin and hair stuck to one end of the cylinder – bits off my scalp!

Jim stood in icy salt water which lapped at his calves. He was still in his sleeping bag, although it had fallen to his knees and twisted around his legs. I felt irritated that he had forgotten to unzip and remove his bag before getting on his feet and that now it was all wet. I was about to tell him so when I noticed my Bill Bryson book was floating face down beside him, along with my pillow, toiletry bag and other sodden objects. I gathered then that Jim hadn't left our bunk voluntarily.

'Yvonne, are you okay?' he yelled, trying to step out of the mass of soggy fabric around his legs and steady himself against the thrashing movement of the yacht. He stumbled across to help me untangle my arms and legs. They seemed to be twisted beneath my body in the oddest of positions.

'You're bleeding,' I gasped. The blood that smeared his face alarmed me as I looked for signs of injury. 'It's *your* blood,' he said, steadying me in a sitting position on the edge of the bunk. 'You've cut your head badly.'

Dave and Andrew appeared, hanging on to a bulkhead to steady themselves as they sloshed through the water towards us. They peered down at me in the same concerned way that Jim had. 'We've rolled,' Jim told me. I could barely hear him through the loud ringing noises in my ears and the roaring of the storm. 'But we're back up again and everything's okay.'

Everything's okay! In a semi-conscious daze I glanced quickly around the cabin and looked back at Jim in disbelief. He couldn't be serious.

The place was a hell of a mess. The inside of the yacht looked like a war zone and was strewn with floating debris. The guys on watch out in the cockpit were half drowned and almost frozen and all of our electronic navigation gear had been knocked out. To top it all off we were just 290 nautical miles off the Antarctic coast, too far south to be reached by any rescue vessel, if we needed one, for days, possibly weeks. Who was he kidding? Everything was clearly far from okay!

The adrenalin and excitement had been building up on board as only hours earlier the force 12 storm of the 'screaming sixties' pushed us before it. The winds had dramatically cranked up to 63 knots and all of a sudden the waves of the Southern Ocean changed, hurling us all over the place at will. Our 19 metre yacht was at the mercy of the weather and battling to survive the vicious seas of the high latitudes. Someone aptly described the monstrous seas that welled up around us as liquid mountains.

Jim and I were sailing north, returning to the civilised world after our year of isolation in Antarctica. Like us, the guys on board were getting more of a sailing adventure than they had bargained on and must have begun to question the sanity of their desire to sail the Southern Ocean. I was firmly convinced that this was not a great way to end our expedition. I was no longer living out my lifelong dream: somewhere, somehow, it had turned into my worst nightmare.

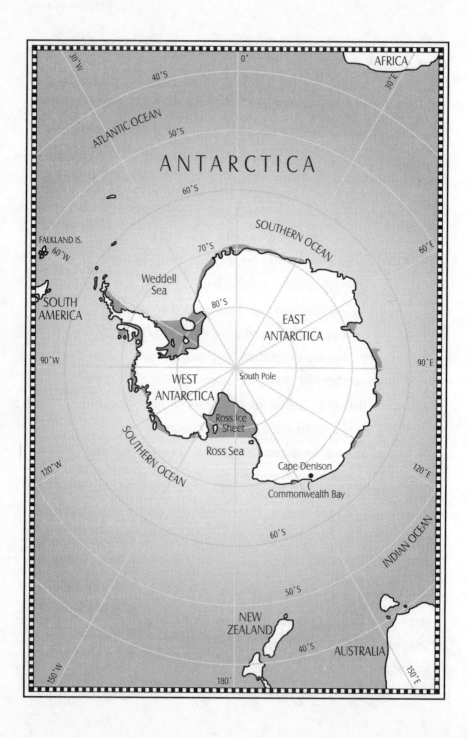

1.

I Want to Go to Antarctica

My Grade 3/4 class of 1995 were hooked. They eagerly crowded around the computer with Marnee and me, watching for the printer to begin chewing out the latest journal from Cape Denison, Antarctica. It was Monday lunchtime. The bell had just gone to signal the end of morning classes and a heated game of four-square had already begun on the asphalt outside the classroom window.

Rats, no response! I keyed in the code again and waited. I was still a novice on the computer and easily bamboozled, so I assumed that I must have typed in an error. Marnee looked over my shoulder as I tried again. This time I paid a bit more attention to hitting the correct keys in the right order and tried to forget about my rumbling stomach. Still nothing.

I could tell that Marnee was beginning to feel a touch uneasy too. Don McIntyre's weekly journal always came through with consistent regularity every Monday lunchtime, and had been doing so ever since we found out about his living in Commonwealth Bay with his wife Margie. Marnee, my teaching partner, and I excitedly registered our classes to receive the McIntyres' unique communications and had evolved a lot of our classroom activities around them. Now I wondered if the couple were okay.

My mind raced through possible reasons why we had not heard from Don, but the most obvious and least worrying one was a glitch in the computer system. It's always easy to blame the computer for problems that crop up. Yet I couldn't help but worry about whether something else had gone wrong. Marnee and I both knew that the hazards of living in the frozen wastes of the world's seventh continent had to be enormous. I shooed the complaining youngsters outside with the assurance that we'd try again after the break.

It was to be another 24 hours before the long-awaited communication came through and we learned that everything was okay and that technology was indeed the reason for the delay. For most of the preceding afternoon, however, I was distracted from my classroom program by thoughts of why Don hadn't sent his usual chirpy and informative message on what had been going on in their life that week. The fact that they had no chance of receiving any assistance or of being evacuated from their remote spot was always a given, but it was only when real trouble became possible that the reality hit home. That night in bed, with no other distractions, I let my mind take me to Antarctica.

As an eight-year-old girl I had my first glimpse of life in Antarctica through a black and white television documentary that showed some of the old footage of Sir Douglas Mawson's Australian Antarctic Expedition of 1911–1914. It had a huge impact on my young and very impressionable mind and to this day I can remember it vividly. The bit of this amazing film that stirred me most was seeing a couple of men attempting to leave the wooden hut in a fierce blizzard to take weather readings from a meteorological screen about 100 metres away. Their clothing was almost torn from their bodies by the fierce katabatic winds that blasted them the minute they were out of the door. At times they disappeared completely from view when the airborne drift engulfed them and they seemed to be absorbed into the Antarctic landscape. I remember watching enthralled as the two men were forced to lean into the wind at a crazy angle in order to make headway, and I was mystified as to why they didn't fall over.

When the scientists returned to the hut their faces and hoods were crusted with a dense layer of ice. The hoods had to be thawed out over the stove before they could be removed, and to my delight the men were laughing.

That was it! I was amazed and excited by what I had seen. My eyes had been opened to a world vastly different from my own small one and I wanted to be a part of it.

Living with three older brothers and two younger sisters in a tiny Housing Commission house in Dandenong, a suburb of Melbourne, had been my entire world. I had never before looked far beyond my own backyard and neighbourhood, and thought that going to school each day was really venturing out. It was when I learned to read that things began to change. Books showed me that there was a world out there beyond my experience, and even beyond my childish dreams. It began to dawn on me that my own environment was in fact a tiny speck on a huge and exciting planet.

As a nine-year-old I avidly read my entire Grade 4 'reader' in the first week of school. It was meant to be the basis of the whole year's literature curriculum and we were discouraged from reading ahead of the class, but I thought it was filled with too many wonderful stories for me to have to wait that long. The one that was most memorable, the one that had the greatest impact on me, was a short excerpt from a book about the successful climb of Mount Everest, the highest mountain in the world. It contained the famous photo of Tenzing Norgay standing on the summit with the Nepalese flag flying from his ice axe in the thin, high altitude air. I was dumbstruck. I didn't know until then that people actually travelled around the world climbing mountains. I wanted to do that too. My imagination was ignited and my daydreams soared to new heights.

One evening at our crowded kitchen table I announced boldly to my family that when I grew up I was going to climb Mount Everest, sail the Southern Ocean and go to Antarctica. My three older brothers just about choked on their mashed potatoes, laughing so loudly. Mum shooshed them then glanced across at me, smiling before turning back to help my younger sisters cut up their food. Dad leaned across the table and said quietly but firmly: 'Yvonne, girls don't do things like that.' What a slap in the face! I was hurt and embarrassed and deeply indignant that I had been dealt such an unfair blow in being born a girl.

Life did a few flips shortly after that. My parents separated and we moved away from the family home to a strange suburb closer to the city, where we lived with Dad and Auntie Betty. That meant a new school, new friends, a new house and a new mum. Our family of eight grew overnight to eleven, as two extra brothers and an older sister joined us. My life as I knew it ceased to exist at that point and a new one began.

Books became even more important to me than before. They provided a distraction from domestic chaos and an escape from city living; best of all they served to nurture my dreams. I read anything I could get my hands on, but I loved adventure stories most. The small amount of weekly pocket money my parents could afford I invariably spent on sweets and books from the secondhand shop on the main road near our house. My brothers' 'Boys Own' manuals had particular appeal as they described stories of explorers and adventurers and far-off places. I craved some adventure in my life. I wanted to experience the extreme and I wanted to see if I could stand up to the challenges that these heroes faced. I couldn't wait to grow up and get out into the real world.

It was to be a long time before I began venturing beyond my safe and comfortable environment, almost 30 years in fact. And if I have any regrets in my life, and I know there are very few, the main one would be that I didn't bite the bullet earlier and get out there and just *do it*!

By 1990 I thought I had everything – Jim, whom I loved passionately and who had been my husband and best friend for 19 years, two delightful sons, a small property in rural Mornington Peninsula, and a great job teaching at a local school. I seemed to have so much and yet it wasn't enough. Deep down I always felt that there was an important ingredient missing – this ingredient I later learned was the key to becoming the real me. I had been a daughter, sister, wife, mother and teacher for so long that I had ignored the importance of being Yvonne as well. There were things I wanted to do just for me, and I decided that if I didn't get a move along I was going to miss my chance.

Following the advice of an 'outdoorsy' friend I joined a local bushwalking club. Within a few months I was off backpacking most weekends and holiday breaks. Jim caught the bug too and together we discovered the beauty of the Australian bush and loved escaping into it every chance we had. Our growing awareness of how insignificant humans really are in relation to the wilderness made it easy to forget the petty worries and frustrations of our small world. Our gradual understanding of the nuances of the environment meant that we were learning to be in touch with our natural surroundings as well as ourselves. I was convinced that there was more to life than striving for the comforts and pleasures, and behaving as if life goes on forever.

It took some time before we could afford to buy all of the latest bushie gear as everything was so incredibly expensive. We were advised to wait until we could buy the better quality brands as they would serve us for many years, so we bought our outdoor equipment bit by bit as we went along. In the meantime we hired what we had to and managed with what we had.

The first couple of overnighters saw us heading off enthusiastically to Wilsons Promontory and to Falls Creek. My hired pack was always far too large for my small frame and rubbed raw spots off the skin covering my tailbone. I didn't know how to adjust all of the straps on the pack and was too shy to ask, so I generally carried it the way I found it. By the end of the day I was usually trailing the group and walking into camp hunched over and desperate to shed my hated load. No wonder my shoulders and back used to take days to recuperate after every walk – just in time to load up and head off again. It wasn't until I acquired my own pack that I realised how comfortable they can be. Once it was fully adjusted to my size and shape I was amazed at the difference. The straps no longer cut into my shoulders; there were no more sores on the bottom of my spine. I also learned that you don't just stuff everything into the pack with the simple aim of getting everything in – an impossible task sometimes. The trick is to distribute the weight so that it doesn't work against your natural posture. What a revelation! Now all I had to learn was how to get the thing up onto my back when there wasn't a rock ledge or something to stand it on first.

Bushies love to talk about their gear. Often at night, lounging around the candle after dinner, the conversation would turn to who had what brand, how much it weighed and how it performed. I always listened to these dialogues in the dark with fascination as the mysteries of Gore-Tex and gaiters, fuel stoves and Sigg bottles were revealed to me. I discovered rather quickly why we struggled more than most over the 15 kilometre days, particularly if there were hills to be trudged up. It turned out that it wasn't a reflection on our fitness or stamina after all, but that our packs weighed nearly twice as much as everyone else's. Lightweight down sleeping bags and special backpacking tents were only a dream for Jim and me in those days, so we had to lug around our old synthetic camping bags and any tent that we could hire or borrow.

In the early days we had a lot to learn about reducing the weight in our packs in every way possible. The idea was to take only the bare necessities, calculate exactly how much food and fuel you would need, remove all packaging, cut the handle off your toothbrush (or better still not take one at all) and not be tempted to pop anything extra in 'just in case'. We heard that everyone took port along for those very social after-dinner chats beneath the stars. We were most popular on the first walk when we produced a whole bottle of our favourite drop instead of a nip or two in a small container, which we quickly learned was the way to go.

Soon Jim and I began to learn how hard we could push ourselves in order to reach those isolated and special places that few people ever venture to. I always thought it was worth the hard slog and was prepared to put my head down and grit my teeth to climb the biggest hills for the best views. My world opened up enormously as I continued challenging myself physically and mentally through the great outdoors.

Our desire to see nature at its best often meant seeing it at its most extreme too. For us it became compelling. I became convinced that anyone could do extraordinary things in their life if they just had the will and were prepared to take some risks. I learned to kayak down rivers and to climb both rock and ice. I can't say that it was always easy, or that I was a natural at any of it. I was often scared witless, but my desire to do these things was so strong that I had to adopt the philosophy of 'feel the fear but do it anyway'. Opportunities were presenting themselves and I was prepared to put in the hard grunt and persistence to make the most of them. I was spending time in awesome places, not only in Australia but in other parts of the world too. Nepal was my favourite and I have been lucky enough to trek and climb there three times. Best of all I was sharing my adventures with an equally enthusiastic Jim.

I knew that I was more than ready to break out of my current lifestyle and go for something really adventurous and different. I had been chipping away at Jim for quite some time with great ideas like teaching in Mongolia for a year or bike riding through Europe. Although none of these received the response I'd hoped for, he never laughed at my dreams.

Early in July 1998 a friend rang suggesting that we buy a copy of that morning's *Herald Sun*. He said that there was a small article in the middle section of the paper that might interest us. It didn't take long to find what he was referring to. It was a brief article on Don and Margie McIntyre who were appearing at the Melbourne Boat Show that weekend in Jeff's Shed (the Melbourne Exhibition Centre). During the interview they'd mentioned that Gadget Hut, the tiny prefabricated box they had lived in in Antarctica three years before, was vacant and available to anyone who'd like to move in.

Gadget Hut is one of the most remarkable dwellings in the world. It is the only privately owned hut in Australia's Antarctic Territory and, possibly, the entire frozen continent. It stands by itself in one of the most isolated locations on earth and despite its miniature size has withstood the toughest Antarctic conditions over the past few years. It looks remarkably like a little cubby house perched by itself on the edge of Commonwealth Bay. It is made of high density foam sandwiched between plywood and fibreglass and is modelled on a kangaroo carcass chiller used in the Australian outback. The hut's dimensions are only 3.6 metres long by 2.4 metres wide, which is not much bigger than the average bathroom. It is chained securely to the rocks on Cape Denison and is about 400 metres from where Mawson's Hut stands. Gadget cannot be seen from the historical area as it is tucked behind a high rocky outcrop to the north-east of the site.

My heart rate began to accelerate as I read the article. My mind raced back to all those months I had followed Don's journals with my class and the wonderful integrated program I'd based around them. That was probably one of my best years of teaching and I knew it was because I was evolving the entire curriculum around something I was passionate about – Antarctica! All the thoughts and dreams I had had about how I would do things if I were in Antarctica instead of Don and Margie flashed through my mind again.

I looked at Jim when I finished reading the article and immediately thought I detected a hint of a spark in his eyes too. I bit the bullet, stared him right in the face, and asked: 'How would you like to spend twelve months with me in a tiny hut in the coldest, windiest place on earth, totally isolated from the rest of the world and beyond rescue?'

How could he resist?

My heart sank as he burst out laughing, but when he stopped and said, 'Yep, let's do it', I knew that we were going to Antarctica.

We chatted excitedly for hours, raving wildly about all the things we could do during our year there. Everything seemed possible at that time, our imagination being our only limit – inland treks up on to the polar plateau, filming documentaries and writing books. We speculated what it would be like to live in freezing temperatures among colonies of Adelie penguins and Wedell seals and not to see another soul for twelve months.

The time out from the rat race had a definite appeal, as did seeing icebergs, auroras and crevasse-filled glaciers. Jim and I were aware that we would be going to a unique place on earth that hadn't yet lost its pristine nature. Everything seemed wonderful and suddenly so attainable. I don't remember getting much sleep that night. We talked and laughed continuously, high on the idea of launching into the biggest adventure of our lives and at the same time totally oblivious to the immense task of mounting a major expedition to Antarctica.

School holidays had just begun and we were in the throes of renovating our house. Our neat, orderly home looked like a bombsite. While the wall was being removed between the lounge and family room I was pretty keen to occupy myself with anything that would distract me from the squalor and mess. I used that time to begin ratting through our books and magazines looking for anything written about the polar region. I collected all of Don McIntyre's old journals from 1995 and re-read them hungrily. As my eyes darted over the pages, my feelings of excitement intensified. I found that I was placing myself into every situation and every photograph. I was certain that some time soon it would be a reality and that I would be on the frozen continent with Jim and seeing everything first hand.

Cape Denison was to be our destination. It is about 2500 kilometres south of Hobart and is a place of great significance in Australia's Antarctic history. It was chosen by Sir Douglas Mawson, the leader of the 1911–1914 Expedition, as the site for their base. The large wooden hut that 18 expeditioners constructed and occupied for two years is still on the Cape, although in a sad state of deterioration due to the effects of nine decades of horrendous weather. Sir Douglas called the place the 'kingdom of blizzards' after discovering that the average daily wind speed over the year was 80 km/h. The highest wind speed recorded for the area is 320 km/h. It has been named as the windiest place on earth. Mawson claimed it was an accursed land and he and his men struggled each year with unrelenting storms hurling barrages of ice and snow. None of this put me off, but only served to make the idea seem more exciting.

At first, we saw the trip as just an entrancing adventure, the fulfilment of a dream to experience Antarctica. I particularly wanted to discover what an Antarctic winter was really like. In all my dreams of journeying down south I had never seen myself travelling there as a tourist. I couldn't bear to go to such an extraordinary place and just look around. I wanted the full experience of what Antarctica had to offer, and that had to include its best and worst. Visiting in summer during the tourist season would only allow me to see the blue skies and the conditions associated with the milder weather. I knew that that wouldn't come anywhere near to showing me the essence of what Antarctica was all about. I wanted to be there when the seasons changed; to watch the wildlife complete their breeding cycle and be forced far out on to the pack ice to survive the winter blizzards. I wanted to watch the last sunset as the 24 hour darkness descended, to be surrounded by a mid-winter blizzard, and to watch the sea freeze over as the continent settled into a long period of hibernation. I thought that the only way to ensure this would be to live there through the full cycle of seasons ... Antarctica, warts and all!

We learned pretty quickly that what we were endeavouring to do wasn't as simple and straightforward to arrange as a year's visit to England might be, and it became obvious that it wasn't exactly mainstream travel either. Just *preparing* for the year in Antarctica was going to be an adventure in itself. Most expeditions south take a year or two in the planning but we didn't have that luxury – we had only a few months in which to make it happen. Even at an early stage it had all the signs of becoming an epic and we were soon to learn that it was going to be quite a character-building experience. We would often be frustrated by the ridiculously short time frame for organising everything, but we were determined not to be beaten by it.

I nervously rang Don McIntyre and told him of our interest in spending a year in the hut in Antarctica. I didn't know whether he would take me seriously or dismiss the idea out of hand. I shouldn't have worried, as I barely got a word in. Don spoke passionately about his own expedition and reeled off lots of fascinating and essential information. It all seemed to flow out of the telephone in one long sentence and I struggled to take it all in. My note-taking skills were severely put to the test, my pages of notes became a mass of scribbled key words, brief phrases and arrows. I managed, however, to get down the all important sequence of steps to be undertaken before Don and Margie could consider becoming involved.

I felt so excited! It all looked so achievable to me – with lots of planning and hard work, of course. I couldn't wait for Jim to get home from work. We had so much to talk about, if only I could decipher my notes. Over the next week Jim and I applied ourselves to the serious task of outlining in writing our background and skill levels, motivation, health status and plans for the year down south and afterwards. We completed these profiles individually, feeling that that was better. I roughed out my piece quickly and without hesitation – after all, I had been thinking about going to Antarctica nearly all my life so it was easy for me. Jim was more thoughtful and reflective. I posted the information off immediately to Don and Margie, hoping they'd be convinced that it wasn't all just a whim.

We must have sparked more than mere curiosity because we heard from Don within days and began a series of long information-sharing phone conversations. Jim set up a conference line so that he and I could both participate in the talks, each of which left our brains at saturation point well before we finished. We took copious notes to help us remember the details later, trying not to be overcome by the many hurdles and obstacles that Don described.

At their invitation Jim and I drove the twelve hours to Sydney to meet Don and Margie early in August. We didn't know what to expect, but right from the first welcoming handshake we were bowled over by their friendliness and their openness and honesty.

Although financially the McIntyres had much to gain by signing us up and sending us on our way south, they didn't ever try to pressure us into going. In fact, quite the contrary, they tried to put us off. They laboured over the difficulties, hardships, dangers and enormous costs of such an adventure. They left us in no doubt that planning and implementing the expedition would be tough and would require a huge commitment and effort. 'Your lives will never be the same again,' they warned.

As we fired questions at them we knew that they were carefully sussing us out, deciding whether we had what it took. They needed to be convinced that we had the skills, experience, personality and drive to survive and enjoy a year alone in Antarctica before they would allow us to 'come on board'.

The McIntyres' own private expedition of 1995 had met the stringent criteria that all activities within the Australian Antarctic Division must meet. Lengthy negotiations and environmental assessments later resulted in permission for them to leave Gadget Hut on-site for a further five years. Don had advertised worldwide for couples to spend twelve months in what he'd described as 'the most expensive hotel room in the world'. Apart from hoping to recoup some of their own expedition costs by renting their hut, the McIntyres wanted to provide opportunities for others to seek adventure as well as heighten awareness of the wonders of the frozen wilderness. I was surprised to discover that Jim and I were the only couple to have pursued it this far. I wondered whether there was a message there?

By the end of the weekend Don realised that despite his brutal frankness he hadn't deterred us one bit and that we were keener than ever to go, so we began to talk about the terms. He explained that if we went ahead with our quest the $100 000 hut rental fee would also cover transportation to and from Cape Denison in their 19 metre yacht and all the help, advice and support they could give us.

Jim and I had kept glancing across the table at each other throughout the entire proceedings. The glint in Jim's eyes and the secret winks he gave me said that he was not wavering in his determination. But in any case Don finally suggested a 'cooldown period' of one week in which we could clearly and objectively make our decision. So, after hugs and handshakes all round, we headed home again. Our heads were spinning with all the further warnings, recommendations and advice. I don't remember talking much for the first couple of hundred kilometres out of Sydney. I relished the opportunity to mull over everything in my mind and to try to sort through what was ahead of us.

The suspense of waiting for final approval by Don and Margie to occupy Gadget Hut, as well as approval by our bank of a loan to begin covering costs, was excruciating. While Antarctica became the focus of every moment of every day, we still hadn't told anyone about our dreams and plans in case they didn't come off. The pressure of keeping such an enormous secret to ourselves was driving us nuts! There seemed to be an awful lot of hurdles to clear before we knew that the trip was a goer – so much could go wrong. What if we couldn't raise the funds or were swamped by the magnitude of the project, or if the McIntyres thought we weren't up to the task and refused to support us? I preferred to wait for the time when Jim and I knew it was definitely happening before we broke the news.

That time came in mid-August. Approval and unlimited support came from the McIntyres and the bank okayed our loan. Our house no longer belonged to us but we couldn't have been happier. This was it – we were going to Antarctica!

One very important hurdle that we had to face immediately was obtaining permission from the Australian Antarctic Division to stay on the continent. To get this we needed to quickly come to grips with the very important issue of how our presence might impact on that environment. I read somewhere that Antarctica is the only continent left on earth that can remind us of how clean the planet should be. We knew that the Antarctic ecosystem is easily disturbed and we wanted to ensure that we didn't damage it in any way. Environmental protection in Antarctica is governed by the Antarctic Treaty system that came into force in 1961. It lays out ways of avoiding pollution of the marine environment and of conserving the local wildlife. We were heading for Australian Antarctic Territory and every aspect of our planned activities had to conform to the *Antarctic Treaty (Environment Protection) Act 1980*.

An Environmental Impact Statement for our proposed 1999 expedition was prepared on our behalf by Don McIntyre. The statement clearly outlined our awareness and understanding of the details of the Treaty and that all facets of our expedition had been carefully planned to conform to the regulations of the Treaty system and the Madrid Protocol. This meant that we had to explain in careful detail our likely impact on the flora, fauna and ecological processes, how our presence would affect the ice, air and surface quality, and what our likely impact on the heritage area of the Cape might be. After careful consideration by the powers that be we were notified that our visit was 'likely to have no more than a negligible impact on the environment' and we were given approval for a year on Cape Denison.

2.

No Time to Work

The announcement to our sons that we were about to pack up the family home and head south for a year could perhaps have been better timed – our 21-year-old Ben had arrived home only that day after six months of backpacking across Europe and had much to tell us about. The five of us, including our other son Ryan (25) and new daughter-in-law Bronwyn, were celebrating with a Mexican feast at a local restaurant. This has been our family tradition when one of us has returned from overseas and we've had many memorable moments over a shared plate of spicy Nachos and a cold beer. After hearing some of the stories of Ben's fabulous travels through eight countries in Europe we decided to tell them about our own impending trip.

'Shiiiiit!' was Ben's loud and spontaneous response when we broke the news. Ryan sat back in his chair and laughed, while Bronny looked as though she thought we were kidding. None of this fazed us: we knew our boys well enough to know that they'd be right behind us once the idea sank in. It didn't take long. They all began talking at once, asking a million questions and ordering more beer. They finished by saying: 'Go for it.'

Later that night, as I lay in bed thinking about leaving the boys behind for what would probably seem like a lifetime, I realised that neither of them had asked why. They both said they weren't surprised and had thought we'd eventually get around to doing something like this. Ryan and Bronny solved Ben's forthcoming homeless problem by suggesting that he move in with them for the year. What great kids!

'Yvonne, I can't believe you're going to Antarctica – you hate the cold!' was Mum's incredulous response when we called in at her unit and told her of our plans. 'And why do you have to go for a year anyway?' She thought that a short holiday of a few weeks would be just as good, we could get Antarctica out of our systems and wouldn't have to go through so much upheaval. It was obvious to us that she was concerned about Jim and me leaving for twelve months, and our explanation of why it had to be for that period didn't make it any easier for her to accept.

There was another thing. Given the difficult ice conditions that are normally present in the Cape Denison region, sailing through in a vessel that was only ice-strengthened, not an icebreaker, required considerable care. Late December and January were the most likely months when a yacht could get into or out of Commonwealth Bay. The time frame for safe sailing was very limited and if the yacht overstayed its welcome it might have to spend the winter there, trapped on the southern side of an impenetrable pack ice. I have heard the area between Commonwealth Bay and Cape Adare, which is on the tip of the Ross Sea, called 'the forbidden coast', because the sea ice often denies access to the region, even at the height of summer.

We didn't know if we should tell Mum at this point that after arriving on the ice and spending our year on the Cape there were no guarantees that the yacht would find its way through the notorious ice barrier on its return journey in 2000. If all efforts failed to reach us after a reasonable time the yacht would be forced to turn back to Australia and leave us there for another year. We were preparing meticulously for that eventuality. Jim and I were sure that Mum would be praying overtime on our behalf from now on and we were happy to get any assistance we could.

Once we started to tell people about our plans, Jim and I used to rate their reactions from one to ten. We called this the 'Wow factor', as almost without fail the first response to our story was 'Wow!' Although a lot of people thought that we were crazy, and said they couldn't think of anything worse than being stuck in a tiny hut with their partner in the depths of Antarctica for a year, every one of them admitted that it was a great adventure and that we should go for it.

Now we had to get our skates on, because we were aiming at a 28 December departure date and that was only four months away. We were planning to leave from Bluff on the southern tip of New Zealand and we had a mountain of things to do before then. I felt very switched on and ready to take on anything!

The next few months were to be a blur of activity. Both Jim and I vastly underestimated the size of the task ahead of us. Fortunately I remembered the old saying: 'The way to eat an elephant is one bite at a time.' That was to be our approach, otherwise we'd be totally overwhelmed. Our first major objective was to conquer the mountain of organisational work necessary to get the expedition underway. We naively thought that we could continue our teaching and training jobs until much later in the year and prepare for the trip after hours. It wasn't long before we realised we had no hope of achieving a December departure date if we didn't put every waking moment into preparing for it.

Graeme Sweatman, the principal of the school in which I worked, was speechless when I revealed my plans. After I responded to what was becoming the standard first question, 'Why?', he generously offered all the support that he could give. He approached the school council on my behalf and made arrangements for me to leave Balnarring Primary School and my Grade 5/6 students in September, which was at the end of term three, for an extended period of leave without pay. 'We want you back again,' he assured me and we tentatively settled on term two in the year 2000 for my return to school.

Three weeks before I left I sent a personal letter home to the families of my students explaining that I wouldn't be returning after the holidays and briefly outlining my plans. I also included an item in the school's newsletter that week to inform the rest of the community. The response was warm and enthusiastic. The morning after I announced that I was off to Antarctica, this beautiful letter arrived at school with a bunch of flowers:

Dear Yvonne,

It was with some hesitation we read your letter outlining your plans for the remainder of 1998 and 1999. We know this is a very exciting time for you and we fully understand your need for leave during fourth term.

However for some of us this will be a time of readjustment. Despite her intelligence and diligence, Courtney will feel deeply your absence in her classroom. In all her years of schooling Courtney has never had a teacher she has connected with in the same way as she has you. You have done so much for her in only three terms. She would have learned, but not with the same confidence.

She will move to high school without doubts but with anticipation. You have made Courtney's last year of primary school one she will never forget. You have done things for her self-esteem no one else was able to do. For all these things we thank you most sincerely.

Of course Courtney is very excited about your expedition and we are sure that she will be an enthusiastic correspondent. We wish you the best of luck for the remainder of the year and especially 1999. We are sure your exceptional experiences will augment the wonderful person you are.

Lynda & Richard

Many other parents and ex-students sought me out to wish me well and offer all sorts of support. Some of the kids from my 1995 grade returned to the school to see me before I left. They were excited that I was now going to Antarctica too and promised to follow my adventure. I knew I would miss the kids and the knack that they have for creating fun in my life.

Jim resigned from his position as a training manager in October and we threw ourselves into making our crazy dream into a well-organised and safe expedition. We worked around the clock.

As more people heard about our plans the offers of assistance and advice poured in. We were amazed! We had thought that only our family and friends would choose to be involved with our adventure, but this wasn't so. Antarctica is an acutely public domain and we learned that almost half of Australia was at some stage interested in what we were planning to do down there. We seemed to have captured the imagination of so many and they all wanted to be a part of it in some way. Their enthusiasm was contagious and Jim and I fed off this as the time raced by and the task of preparing seemed to increase in size the further we got into it.

We began to see that there was great value in what we were doing, not only for ourselves but for a large number of unknown people too. We considered the possibility of continuing to share the adventure with others once we were actually stationed on the ice. I wondered: 'Why should we have all the fun?' That was when the concept of 'Expedition Antarctica – Share the Journey' was launched and Murray Foster joined our team of enthusiastic and hardworking individuals.

My sister Vicky and her husband Steve introduced Murray to us with the thought that he might be able to help set up some marketing strategies to assist in selling our expedition and its story to potential sponsors. We discovered that his greatest asset was his ability of standing back and looking at the big picture, while Jim and I tended to become bogged down with too many details. When Murray came on board, offering his services and expertise, our expedition began to really take shape. We were a little scared, particularly as everything had to move along so quickly, but we were committed and determined to keep moving forward.

Our notion of adventure had always related to the outdoors. Adventure to us was an endeavour that was physically and mentally challenging, that put us out of our comfort zone and required resilience, determination and a lot of problem-solving ability. We soon found that this concept had a far greater application than merely trekking the Himalayas or kayaking a swollen river. Establishing our own company, Adventures in Education, was a huge undertaking for us and held all the elements of true adventure. We were faced with learning about and implementing business plans, Gantt charts, event management, sponsorships and contracts. We realised that the journey had already begun as Jim, Murray and I spent long days and endless nights talking things through over countless cups of lemon tea and slabs of fruitcake, trying to get a handle on events. Our learning curve was steep as we found there was so much that we had to consider, learn, understand and apply if we were going to do this thing properly. We were now a long way from merely buying a year's worth of food, some nice warm clothes and a camera and sailing to Antarctica.

Jim is a great organiser. After 26 years of marriage I already knew that, but it was in watching him kick into action at the planning stages of the expedition that I fully appreciated his talent. I always used to make fun of his predisposition for making lists. I preferred to operate from memory, finding lists tiresome and something else to worry about. Jim, alternatively, gained a great deal of pleasure from the act of compiling lists as much as he did from ticking each item off once accomplished. It became apparent very early in the piece that lists were going to be a major tool in our preparation phase if we were to arrive in Antarctica well equipped and well organised.

From day one Jim set himself up in front of the computer and began preparing databases and spreadsheets for every component of the expedition. These he diligently upgraded and amended on a regular basis, printing them off and presenting them to me for perusal and feedback. I was staggered to find that every aspect of the planning phase was being carefully documented and electronically filed. As I handed him my hand-scrawled notes and lists on odd scraps of paper he would receive them with an annoyingly patronising look and proceed to put them into yet another file on his computer before we discussed the contents.

By mid-October things were starting to take shape. Our basic plan was firm, the legal and financial details clear, and we even had an expedition logo. Murray began approaching potential sponsors who could help us to achieve a major goal of the expedition – to share the journey with as many people as possible. Initial reactions were very encouraging and bolstered our confidence and belief in what we were doing.

Andrew Hocking, a senior project officer in the learning technology section of Vic Ed, scored a 'Wow factor' of almost ten when he learned about our plans. He immediately saw the potential for using our adventure as a focus for a 'Global Classroom' project. The possibility of establishing a partnership with the Victorian Department of Education was a big thrill for me. The chance to take school children from every corner of Australia with us on our twelve month journey electrified me. I would have the biggest class in Australia, maybe the world!

A large part of Andrew's role in the department was to encourage the use of computer technology in learning activities across the curriculum and at all levels in Victorian schools. I remembered the great times my grade and I had shared with the McIntyres. Now it seemed I was going to be able to offer the same opportunities to others, and much more. This time it could be very high tech, and with the availability of computers and the Internet to most children through their schools we could make the experience interactive too. With the right equipment and training Jim and I could regularly send diaries and photos back to a website, as well as snippets of video footage. We could directly receive and send communications to classes and individuals, and also arrange regular satellite phone links. The possibilities were astounding and I knew deep down that if nothing else was achieved on this trip this project would make it all worthwhile.

After the initial meeting at the offices of Vic Ed in Melbourne we were encouraged by an invitation to return and talk more about establishing an Internet program together and to meet Andrew's offsider, Nikki. We learned much later that one of Nikki's roles in that meeting was to be Andrew's 'crap meter'. She had to help him to decide if Jim and I were for real and could genuinely deliver and participate in such a big project.

We arrived at the second meeting with all of the profiles, background information, outlines, data and details that they'd asked for, neatly presented in triplicate and proudly displaying the expedition logo. Apparently we passed with flying colours and the 'Share the Journey – The Claypoles' Journey to Antarctica' educational website was born.

We were to work closely with the project officers from Curriculum Development and Learning Technologies to develop extensive online teaching and learning materials. Students from P–10 (prep to Year 10) were to be our target group and they would be able to access a wide range of online classroom activities designed to encourage and stimulate their learning about Antarctica. Jim and I followed themes such as survival, the environment, history and technology. A very cute virtual penguin named Claypole the Penguin was created. The idea was that I would write little diaries each week telling about his adventures on Cape Denison. I hoped that he would appeal to the younger children and that they would learn a lot about Antarctica through their special little feathered friend.

Committing ourselves so heavily in a financial sense created the most stress for us. We had always been conservative in our approach to handling money and we were proud of our financial achievements over the years. At the time that this idea came into our lives we were fairly well off and able to enjoy spending some of our hard-earned cash on ourselves. Suddenly we were plunged right back to the early days of our marriage when we were struggling to pay the bills. Jim and I had to have a lot of faith and to believe that if something was meant to be it will be. The expedition was falling neatly into place and it was generating a great deal of interest and support from surprising areas. We knew that we couldn't just stop now. With our own financial commitment, and that of some major corporations, we would get there. It just wasn't going to be easy.

Potential sponsors who had been captivated by our expedition suddenly began to offer us more than encouragement. Many supported the educational component of the expedition and loved the spirit of adventure shown by two ordinary Australians. By the end of November we had major sponsorship deals with the magazine *New Idea*, Telstra and NSA Juice Plus. Each of these major companies became very involved in Expedition Antarctica and we formed warm friendships with many of the people in each organisation.

Terry Chalmers at Telstra Learn IT was keen to get behind us and offered generous assistance with the cost of the satellite phone calls that would let us achieve our goal of reaching a million school children throughout Australia. We knew that the telephone cost of running our schools program from Antarctica could be around the $80 000 mark, so Telstra's support meant that we could proceed without worry.

Macpac helped us with specialised clothing and backpacks, Bogong Equipment provided most of our technical outdoors equipment at much reduced prices, and Sanitarium gave us enough cereal, lentils, dried fruit and nuts to keep us healthy and happy for a year. We were very grateful for everyone's support and felt extremely fortunate to have such strong sponsorship when we knew that these companies were constantly approached for assistance with worthwhile causes.

The enthusiasm of our sponsors in the weeks prior to departure was a real shot in the arm for us. NSA, the Juice Plus company, were excited to have us volunteer to test their dietary supplements in a unique, controlled environment over a long period of time. Kate Bowyer arranged for us to go to the Childrens Hospital in Melbourne to have a series of blood tests before leaving, and planned to repeat those tests soon after our return to discover what effect the supplements had had on our system during the year away. We were provided with a full twelve month supply of Juice Plus capsules and we guaranteed that we would take them religiously twice a day. Although neither of us had ever tried the Juice Plus capsules before we were delighted to have them on the expedition, as they are made from fresh fruit and vegetables and both of those were going to be only a memory once the yacht dropped us off in January. NSA further showed their support for our expedition by providing some much needed cash.

Joining the team at *New Idea* was to be one of the highlights of my whole year. Bunty Avieson, the magazine's editor, loved what we were doing and was very keen for her readers to become part of the expedition. She had envisaged publishing two major stories before departure and two more on our return, as well as series of regular articles directly from Antarctica. It was decided that I would write ten 'letters' for the magazine while I was away, which I thought was pretty gutsy as I had never had anything published before and they might have been a dreadful flop. I knew my Mum and my sister would read them but I couldn't be sure about anyone else. I should have had as much faith in Bunty's intuition as she had in my ability, because as it turned out I wrote 50 full page 'Letters From Antarctica' and *New Idea* published every one of them.

The spillover effect of those articles, in terms of my heightened media profile and the wonderful e-mail response from thousands of readers, was to be totally beyond what any of us had foreseen. Many readers throughout Australia became hooked on our adventure and were right there with us from the days we began packing until we returned safely to Melbourne 13 months later. It was impossible to feel lonely knowing they were all there behind us.

Despite the generous support shown by sponsors, when it came down to the final figures Jim and I covered most of the costs for our expedition. We decided right at the beginning that we would be prepared to mortgage our home to provide the dollars needed. We had to pay the McIntyres $100 000 for the rent of their hut and the yacht trip down and back. We initially calculated that everything else would cost about half that again. An outlay of $150 000 didn't sound too steep for the unique opportunity to live in Antarctica for a year.

As our preparations and spending continued at a cracking pace we realised that we had greatly underestimated the size of the expedition as well as the costs of going to Antarctica with such high goals as ours. Our budget blew right out when we added the computers, the specialised hardware and software, the camera equipment and the satellite B phone. We also decided at that time to engage Murray as project manager for the next twelve months and added his wages to our expenditure chart. We really started to worry when we found ourselves in more debt than we had ever planned and the initial $100 000 looked like small change. We took out another loan, sold off our retirement investments and even considered selling my four-wheel-drive if necessary. There was no turning back; we had to believe that everything would fall smoothly into place eventually, including the money.

During our hectic days of planning and preparation Jim and I were riding on an emotional rollercoaster. The thrill of making a dream come true was always with us. We simply couldn't get Antarctica off our minds, we were eating, sleeping and breathing this adventure. It had simply taken over our lives. At times we had to dig deep to find the tenacity needed to turn our ideas into reality. It was important for us to set short-term goals and then work hard to reach them. We learned from our mistakes and continually motivated ourselves and each other to succeed.

We coped well with the logistics of the preparation, and had fun deciding what we would need for our survival in the harshest of

Antarctic environments. We met a number of people who had spent time on the continent and enjoyed many pleasurable sessions picking their brains for information and tips. Meeting Alan Parker and his lovely wife Jan during our preparation time was a real bonus.

I had met Alan years before when I invited him to talk with my class at school about Antarctica. Alan had been to the continent on many occasions and was once a station leader at Macquarie Island and also at Davis station. He has been rewarded with the Polar Medal for his services to the Australian Antarctic Division, and is a very knowledgeable bloke when it comes to survival down there. I really liked his down to earth manner and rang him in the hope that he could spare us some time so that we could ask his advice about part of our plans.

Alan and Jan were wonderful. They were both very interested in what we were about to do and full of good ideas and encouragement to help us on our way. We visited them a few times in the weeks before departure and were also able to keep a correspondence going with them by e-mail while we were living on the ice. Alan was totally no-nonsense when he spoke about safety and survival. He said that Antarctica is a lovely lady but also wicked. 'She grabs you and draws you in,' he said, 'then cuts you off at the feet!' He warned us never to be tempted to go out onto the sea ice as the winds around Commonwealth Bay are known to blow the ice out suddenly and leave open water. If we were caught out there we would have no chance of surviving. His other stern warning was to exercise rigid self-control in regard to preventing CO poisoning. If anything was going to get us while we were down there it was likely to be something as 'benign' as this. His advice was to never sleep with the heater on, not even in catnaps during the day; to watch the colour of the flame, as yellow meant toxic fumes; and to always vent the hut when burning kero.

When talking about the long winter months Alan said: 'It's not the way you think it's going to be. You will be totally bored out of your minds at some stage.' He told us of the many problems associated with boredom when living in such confined conditions in a hostile environment. I had already read about Richard E. Byrd's experiences with this very real problem back in the early part of the 20th century. He had noted that under such conditions, with not much else to do, men soon learn to take each other's measure.

Byrd wrote: 'In a polar camp little things have the power to drive even the most disciplined men to the edge of sanity.' Alan Parker had seen bunkmates stop talking to each other as they began to detest each other's habits and idiosyncrasies. The way someone left his things lying around or ate his food could become unbelievably annoying. Best mates had become enemies over time. Alan had seen the effects on men living in small communities at the stations, but he couldn't imagine how difficult it would be for the two of us alone.

One of the ideas that Alan suggested to help us get through the year was to find a way to show the passing of time. His suggestion was to divide the year into twelve parts and then to nominate one day each month when we would indulge in a nice meal and a bottle of wine and personal gifts. The gifts would become keepsakes later and would bring back strong memories of exactly what we were doing and feeling at that particular time of year. We loved this idea and spent hours fighting the Christmas crowds, secretly hunting for twelve little gifts to brighten up each other's year. These we wrapped in the lairiest paper we could find, numbered them from 1 to 12, and packed them away safely along with all the other presents we had been given to open on special occasions throughout the year.

Antarctica has no permanent population. Everything required for human survival must be taken there – food, shelter, warmth and a means for melting snow to provide essential water. No one can live off the land in this wilderness, so planning a stay in Antarctica is like preparing for a trip to the moon. Everything has to be thought of and there is little margin for error.

Correspondingly, going to Antarctica is to all intents and purposes like disappearing off the face of the earth. Our entire life had to be put on hold for an extended period of time. We had to move out of our home and place all our belongings into storage as well as find a caring family to occupy the house. We needed to let the house for security reasons and, to be honest, we needed the money too. It is a wrenching experience packing away all of your family's accumulated belongings and depersonalising your home, ready for strangers to move in. Once the photos were removed from the walls, though, I found that the heart seemed to go out of our home and the place lost its character and homeliness.

Taking advantage of this opportunity to get rid of a lot of accumulated junk I made various trips to the local op shop. Jim's 26 years of collecting and hoarding meant that the garage and sheds had quite a lot of stuff that 'might come in handy one day'. No donations to charity there – Jim thought it was all worth keeping.

It took us a month to clear out the house bit by bit, and with our growing collection of expedition equipment we began moving into Mum's small unit with her. This was to be our home and headquarters for December. Poor Mum! She must have felt that her place was being taken over. We filled up her garage first and then the spare bedroom, before spilling into the lounge and dining room. There were mountains of boxes and more turning up every day as our specialised gear began to arrive and we had the task of sorting through it and repackaging the contents.

Mum fed us three huge meals a day, trying to get some meat on our bones before we left. She did our washing, took messages, made calls on our behalf, sewed new doona covers and snugly warm sleeping bag liners, and was generally a terrific calm person to have around during such a hectic time. 'This,' she said, 'is my contribution to the expedition.' We probably couldn't have kept up such a gruelling pace without her looking after us. I don't think she realises to this day what a huge contribution it was and how much we appreciated everything that she did.

Our two Boxer dogs, very much a part of our family for years, needed a foster home. After searching unsuccessfully for months, in desperation I rang the RSPCA for advice. They suggested that I separate them and consider giving them away permanently, or as a last resort have them put down humanely. I was horrified! I knew that I could do neither of those things. Finally, as a last resort, I put my limited computer skills to work and made a 'Foster Parents Wanted' poster. I added what I thought was a gorgeous and irresistible photo of Max and Tiger. My sister said: 'There's no such thing as a gorgeous photo of Boxers, they're just too ugly.' Bemused and sympathetic shopkeepers in the milk bars and general stores of my local area displayed the posters for me and over the next few days I tried not to think of the consequences of not hearing from anyone.

Someone was smiling down from above when Michaela and her daughters saw one of our Wanted posters and rang me at home. I laughed pathetically when Michaela asked if the dogs were still available. She said that she had grown up with Boxers back in Germany and would love to have a few around again. She had already discussed it with her family and they wanted to take them in for the year. We nervously took Tiger and Max to meet their prospective new family, hoping that the boisterous Max would be on his best behaviour. It was love at first sight. Except for Jet the cat, that is – Max took one look at him and I could tell that he wasn't planning to make his life easy. I worried about that poor cat all year, but as it turned out Max came off second best after their first encounter and peace soon reigned again in their home.

During this crazy period of frantic activity our social life inevitably took a back seat. We found that we didn't have time to sit back and enjoy the company of our friends when we wanted to. It dawned on us early in December that unless we made an effort it was going to be a long time before we saw any of them again. We organised a big informal get together at the Flinders Pub one Sunday afternoon and spent a fabulous six hours talking, laughing and sharing a drink with everyone. Their excitement and enthusiasm for our venture was wonderful.

Everyone knew how busy we had been and understood why we had dropped out of the scene. They grilled us for all the latest information on our trip and loved hearing stories like the details of how we calculated our basic provisions. How we worked out the quantity of toilet paper we would need for a year was a favourite. To test this Jim and I took a toilet roll each and used it exclusively until it ran out. Even when we went to the toilet in restaurants or other homes we took our roll with us because in Antarctica there wouldn't be any other conveniences around and we needed an accurate tally of our total need. We kept a record of how long each of our rolls lasted and from that information calculated a year's supply. We worked it out that one roll a week would easily be enough for both of our needs, then doubled it, just to be sure. A nice easy total of one hundred rolls of toilet paper.

Some people were flabbergasted, claiming that they would easily use three times that much and hoping that we didn't bite our nails. A lighthearted and very animated conversation would follow on how many sheets of loo paper everyone thought they would use in a day and if it made a difference whether they were a 'scruncher' or a 'folder'. I hadn't laughed so much in ages.

I knew that we would miss lots of people when we began our time in isolation on the ice. Satellite communications were going to be possible, but technology couldn't replace the warmth and intimacy of face-to-face chats with good friends over a glass of wine. A number of thoughtful people gave us special items to take with us to keep us safe and to remind us that we were in their thoughts. None were more special than the Saint Christopher medals lent to Jim by his mate Terry. They had been blessed by the Pope and had been carried by Terry throughout his active service in the Vietnam War. A highly emotional Jim could do no more than place them carefully in a folder and swear to Terry that he would bring them back.

Five days before leaving Melbourne we were in a tizz of last minute activity, mainly because the equipment for the communications system had only recently arrived from interstate. Our amazing 'techo team',

Steve, Vaughn and John, were flat out checking all the components and setting the system up to ensure that it could do all the things we needed it to.

The day before Jim and I were due to sail down to Tasmania to join the yacht we began our training in operating and maintaining the system. No one had slept much over the past few nights and the day was a stinker, 40°C in the shade. Despite the obvious strain we had all been under, everyone knew that the pressure was on and the excitement was almost tangible. We were all running on adrenalin by then trying to come to grips with the operations of the satellite system and all the components that were to run off it. Vaughn was very patient with me as he attempted to make a self-confessed 'technophobic' into someone who could not only independently use the equipment but also understand the system. My learning curve was nearly vertical, but around mid-afternoon I was confident that I had a basic understanding. Fortunately Jim is a computer whiz and I could be assured of some extra private tuition once we got on to the ice.

We were now alarmed to find that there were still segments of the system not working properly. The techo boys weren't too fazed and were confident of getting to the root of the trouble – in fact, I think they were enjoying the technical challenge. Vaughn was obviously in his element working with leading edge technology and we were indebted to him for his enormous efforts. The task called for another all-nighter, then everything was to be delivered to us by John in the carpark of the ferry terminal the following morning at 5:30. How close to the wire can you get?

As we were thanking the pair for their huge efforts and preparing to leave for our last night at home, Steve turned up unexpectedly. He had with him the newly completed housing, made by his friend Stuart, for the satellite aerial we were going to mount on the outside of Gadget Hut's sloping annex wall. The varnish was still sticky as we practised putting the prefabricated pieces together on Vaughn's front porch. It was bulky and cumbersome but once we thought we had it worked out and were sure that all the screws and seals were there we boxed it up, loaded it into the car and headed back to Mum's place. We still had many hours of final sorting and packing to do before we could consider going to bed and were anxious to get started on it.

We spent a total of two and a half hours in bed that night. The temperature stayed in the 30s. I tried not to get too emotional as I lay there, but I was at the point of exhaustion physically and emotionally and sleep would not come. I was overwhelmed by the heat of the night, the smells of Mum's recently watered garden and the distant sounds of traffic. I wondered if I could keep these things clear in my memory for a whole year.

3.

Medical Nightmare

*A*ntarctica is essentially a germless continent. The seas surrounding it are frozen most of the time, creating a barrier against the germ-laden civilisations of the rest of the world. The only germs that we were likely to encounter were the ones that we took down there with us; even then the frigid temperatures would deal with many of those. We could look forward to a year with little fear of annoying colds and flu or other nasty bugs. As we saw it, though, becoming injured or ill was one of the major threats once we were on our own. The possibilities were very real and had to be prepared for.

Margie McIntyre, who has a nursing background, had equipped Gadget Hut with a comprehensive medical kit. She also upgraded the out-of-date drugs for us. We obtained a list of all the first aid items, lotions and potions and the more serious drugs included in that kit. It was apparent that almost everything that was likely to go wrong in a year was catered for. There were enough equipment and supplies for almost any medical situation that could crop up in Antarctica, and then some. We would have everything available from aspirin to Xylocaine, enemas to pethedine, and artery forceps to naso-gastric tubes – though we didn't know what to do with most of them. A bottle of Dettol, a tube of Savlon and a packet of Bandaids were about the extent of our first aid kit at home.

Fortunately Dr John Roth, our family GP, offered to spend time helping us come to terms with everything. We systematically discussed each item on the list and what it could be used for, as well as how to and when to use it. I made copious notes as he ran through everything. There was so much to know, such as that Xylocaine came in the form of ointment or in ampoules. One type is combined with adrenalin. I noted that Xylocaine is used as a local anaesthetic, and one type stops bleeding as well. The important thing, though, is never to use the one with adrenalin on fingers and toes! I can't remember why, but my notes had a warning written in bold, followed by two exclamation marks, so I knew that it was a serious no-no.

John Roth kept a list of all our drugs in his own files to refer to in the event of our needing a satellite consultation during the year. He recommended that we add some other items to the kit, including supplies of Jim's cholesterol drugs, different antibiotics, throat lozenges, elastic bandages, rolls of cottonwool and plaster of Paris strips. I especially liked the latest Red Cross first aid manual, as it was easy to follow and had plenty of photos rather than drawings. We bought a copy and packed it along with a book covering cold injuries such as frostbite, frozen lung and hypothermia.

When we became involved in outdoor activities Jim and I thought it sensible to learn first aid procedures. We were often away from immediate help and knew that we might be forced to rely on each other in an emergency. Our Level 2 certificates had been kept current over the years and we felt reasonably confident in dealing with the initial response to most accidents, but it was ongoing treatment such as a doctor or hospital provides that was going to be the hard bit in Antarctica.

John patiently showed us how to deal with dislocations and burns, and the basic procedure for setting broken bones. It all seemed so easy being guided along in his comfortable, warm consulting room with the lovely sound of native birds singing in the garden outside the window. We all knew full well, however, that if we were ever required to repeat any of those procedures in Antarctica the circumstances would be quite different. Things would be far more desperate, particularly as the environment could be more dangerous and life threatening than the injury itself.

Don McIntyre suggested that we follow the Antarctic Division's checklist for pre-expedition medicals given to all wintering-over personnel. When I glanced through the items on the checklist I realised that it was certainly comprehensive. We were about to submit ourselves to quite a barrage of tests. None of this put me off as I had always enjoyed great health and was careful with my eating and exercising. I saw the checks as something else to get out of the way, another part of the preparation to be completed and crossed off the list.

Apparently, living in sub-zero temperatures can play havoc with teeth. I have read that teeth can shatter with the cold and fillings have a tendency to loosen or pop out unexpectedly, exposing nerves to icy air as you gasp for breath fighting your way around outside. Thorough dental checks were another thing that had to be endured in the hope that we would return home with our mouths in the same state as when we left. Jim made many visits to have old fillings replaced and one of his molars rebuilt. On the final visit he was given two tiny tubes of temporary filling – 'just in case ...' I wasn't sure whether to be delighted with the dentist's thoughtfulness or to wonder if he lacked confidence in his own handiwork. We packed those tiny tubes in a bag where we could be sure we'd find them if they were needed. It wasn't until months down the track that we realised we hadn't received any instructions with the filling material or any tools for applying it!

The appendix is another part of the human anatomy that can be seriously affected by the cold. All Australian personnel spending a year in any part of Antarctica where there is no surgical unit and doctor available are required to have their appendix removed beforehand. In 1961 a Russian doctor self-diagnosed a possible perforated appendix and some localised infection. He was stationed off the coast of Queen Maude Land and was unable to be evacuated due to the horrendous weather. He proceeded to operate on himself, using a local anaesthetic, with the help of the meteorologist who managed the surgical retractors and of another expeditioner who held a mirror so that the doctor could see what he was doing. Reports say that the doctor was back on duty inside two weeks.

My appendix was removed when I was 14 years old, but Jim still had his intact. Although I assured him that I was willing to hold a mirror for him if he had to perform his own surgery in Gadget Hut he declined the offer and arranged to have the operation. Everything went smoothly and he was home, a bit sore and sorry for himself, two days later. I made up a bed for him on the couch for the first couple of nights because the tidal waves created by our waterbed every time one of us moved caused him to roll about in agony.

While we fully appreciated how important it was to leave on our adventure in peak physical condition, we also had to consider our mental and emotional health. We both knew that in every respect, particularly the psychological side, the risks surrounding our expedition were very real. Jim and I would be jammed together in a small hut, rarely able to be more than a few paces from each other. During the long dark winter the wind and the cold would prevent us from leaving the hut for days on end. Each day would eventually become a repeat pattern of the day before, the week before, one barely distinguishable from the other. We knew that our survival could depend on our ability to dig deep inside ourselves for hidden levels of motivation to outlast such an ordeal.

Monotony and claustrophobia, along with isolation and deprivation, were going to be a test of our mental stamina, but the addition of living in total darkness for weeks over winter could only compound the difficulties. Various studies have taken place on the effects on people as the winter days become darker. It seems that some suffer depression as the lack of light interferes with the production of brain chemicals such as melatonin. One weather observer on Macquarie Island is well known for his slogan: 'Every bastard down here is mad except me!' These people typically feel fine again in summer when the sun returns.

Winter was the time I was looking forward to most. It was my main reason for spending a year in Antarctica. I knew that living in a box in a harsh, isolated and extremely cold environment increased the likelihood of anxiety and depression but I was excited by the opportunity to find out how I would measure up. Did I have what it took to get through such a challenge? I was confident that I did and was keen to discover exactly what mood swings and changes I would go through as the year progressed. Jim and I are adaptable and don't mind putting up with a fair bit of discomfort in order to achieve something that we consider worthwhile. So we weren't as concerned about the hardships we were submitting ourselves to as many other people around us were.

The psychological risks associated with such a year argue against a group of less than three. Three is seen as the classic number. Richard E. Byrd believed that three would 'balance each other like the legs of a tripod'. After 26 years of marriage Jim and I had a very close relationship and didn't think that we would have too many difficulties with our unusual situation in Antarctica. Ever since we have known each other we have never fought, preferring to talk things through before they reach the explosive point. We've spent a lot of time in each other's company because we prefer it that way, often to the exclusion of others. Over the years we've come to understand each other's needs well and so we believed we could support each other when the going got tough at the hut.

Lack of personal space and privacy was inevitable living in such a small enclosed space. I knew there would be times when the blizzards would pound the Cape relentlessly and not allow us to get outside. We could be confined in the hut for long periods of time. I came up with the idea that we'd take our own portable CD player and headphones. If either of us had a need to be alone then putting on the headphones would signal that we wanted time out. That meant no talking, touching or eye contact the whole time the headphones were on.

The problems faced by people in the polar regions, particularly the problems associated with isolation and living and working in confined areas, are also experienced by space crews. We had heard of studies aimed at enhancing the performance, health and safety of those in such unusual settings. Dr Gary Steel of the Lincoln University in New Zealand heard about Jim and me and asked if we would be willing to participate in one such study. Gary works closely with NASA and individuals at the McMurdo Antarctic Station. He liked the idea of being able to monitor a couple living in extreme conditions of cold, minimal space, loneliness and total isolation. We completed a lengthy personality profile days before leaving Australia and agreed to fill out POMS (Profiles of Mood State) each month throughout our stay.

Our visits to a psychologist and a psychiatrist shortly before leaving helped us to visualise a number of scenarios that we might be forced to deal with. We were encouraged to work through ways of dealing with them before we left home. The idea was that if we had already talked our way through a number of possible situations then they would be easier to handle if and when they actually arose. The one that startled me most, probably because it had never occurred to me before, was what we would do if one of us sustained a serious injury or illness and was living in virtually intolerable pain month after month. I knew that we had a variety of pain-killing drugs in the medical kit, but they were only for short-term fixes. What would we do? The thought was frightening. Some training in self-hypnosis was recommended but our tight time line before departure made that impossible; the best we could do was to buy an audio relaxation tape. It had to be another of those things that we hoped like hell wouldn't occur ... but if it did, well, we'd have to deal with it somehow!

The last item on my medical checklist was a mammogram. It was listed as optional for all wintering-over females, and as time was marching on and I still had so much to do I was tempted not to bother with it. Jim disagreed firmly and said: 'Why take the risk? Make the time or you might be sorry.'

Through the local Breast Screen clinic I arranged to have an X-ray done late in September. I squeezed the appointment in between another meeting with Vic Ed and a trip to the dietitian who was going to look over our food lists. The X-rays were quickly completed and without further thought I stepped out of the consulting rooms and raced for the city to keep my next appointment. However, a phone call a week or so later informed me that something had shown up on the mammogram that needed following up. I was stunned but tried not to let the 'what ifs' take hold. The person I rang to make the new appointment assured me that most call-backs reveal nothing sinister or nasty and that I wasn't to worry.

My appointment was at the Monash Medical Centre, about 85 kilometres from home. I drove myself over and Jim went to work. This was one of his last days before leaving his job to concentrate full time on the expedition so there was a lot happening in the office at the time.

My original X-ray showed a light patch on my right breast that shouldn't have been there. Further X-rays were taken to magnify that area for closer examination. Then I was sent to another waiting room to wait some more. I sat looking at the three women already sitting there silently. All of them wore the same floral hospital gown as I did. Each had a plastic basket on the floor beside her containing the items of clothing she had just shed for her mammogram.

I wondered what was going through their minds as they sat waiting. It was hard to tell as everyone carefully avoided making eye contact, as if not wanting to be associated with the scene. We all sat quietly waiting, hoping that we weren't going to be confronted with the shattering news of the discovery of a malignant lump growing within our bodies.

The three women were led out to other examination rooms and I was left alone for a while. My self-talk was positive, but a small knot was beginning to form in my stomach. I tried to distract myself with a crossword puzzle that I found in a *New Idea* – but who was I kidding? I couldn't do those things even when I was completely relaxed and had nothing more on my mind than what wine I was going to have with dinner.

A nurse appeared and took me down the corridor for an ultrasound investigation of the suspect area. This didn't sound good to me and I reluctantly followed her into another procedure room in a different part of the hospital. That was when things began to happen so quickly that the details became a bit of a blur. Another doctor was consulted after the ultrasound and biopsies and aspirations were ordered. By that time there were four doctors and nurses crowded in the room with me. Someone briefly explained what they were planning to do as they hurriedly began swabbing a large area of my breast and a nurse arranged the shiny cold instruments of torture on a tray beside the table. Samples of tissue were going to be removed for closer examination in the laboratory. I lay on the table trying to relax but the procedures were very painful and unpleasant, particularly by the time they got to the sixth one. I didn't think that I had enough breast tissue to be able to spare that much!

Suddenly I felt totally overwhelmed by what was happening. It was all becoming a bit too serious and I wanted Jim with me. Tears started pouring down my face and thought I was going to throw up. A nurse, seeing my distress, sponged my face gently to cool me down as she tried to reassure me that it was nearly over.

When I finally got off the table and was dressed again I sat in the nurse counsellor's office sipping coffee and trying to keep the tears in check. Jenny had a lovely caring manner but I didn't want it because it made me feel that I had already been diagnosed with cancer, and her gentle tone made me blubber even more. Perhaps I needed someone with a sergeant major's approach, someone who would dish out the facts in an abrupt and no-nonsense manner. My thoughts and emotions were all over the place and I wanted it all to go away like a bad dream.

Fighting the urge to run out of the medical centre, I calmly walked through the waiting room and headed for the comfort and seclusion of my car. I realised that my life now had the potential to take a very dramatic turn and undergo a profound change. The brief three hour period that I spent undergoing tests may have been the signal for that unwanted change, and I was scared out of my wits.

Pathology rushed the test results through. All of the staff knew that I was leaving for Antarctica in December and promised to help speed things up where possible. The following two days and nights dragged by as I struggled to come to terms with what I perceived as a terrible threat to my dreams, if not to my life. I pushed my mind to stay in control and not to even contemplate the 'what ifs'. It sounds easy but it wasn't. Something like that was hard to ignore, it tended to take over. Everything that was going on in the world suddenly seemed unimportant. I didn't want to do anything and I couldn't sleep. It was hard to let my mind go long enough to allow sleep to take over. Jim calmly tried to reassure me but I had a sense that he was feeling some concern too. I told no one else, and the stomach knot grew bigger and bigger.

Jim and I returned to the medical centre together. I was so glad that I wasn't alone this time as I had a horrible feeling deep down that I wasn't about to hear good news. I wasn't being unduly pessimistic, but after being asked to submit to all those extra tests I felt that the odds must have been against me. My self-talk had ceased and my mind was numb as I sat holding Jim's hand in a vice-like grip, waiting for the final results.

A doctor suddenly appeared in the room. He sat down opposite us, introduced himself and said: 'Mrs Claypole, I'm afraid that your tests show you have a malignant spot on your right breast.' My weak response was: 'Does that mean I have breast cancer?'

I almost felt a sense of relief at hearing those awful words: 'Yes, you have breast cancer.' That seemed such a ridiculous thing to think but at least now I knew, and the deep, empty black days of waiting were over. I relaxed the grip on Jim's hand and the blood rushed back into his knuckles. My stomach knot was gone. I was amazed that I responded to the shattering news with such calm. Perhaps I had been expecting it and now that it was confirmed I felt I could begin setting my mind to dealing with it. Or maybe I was just in shock and my reaction was going to surface later.

Jim sat beside me in stunned silence. I began a barrage of questions. I figured that if I was to get rid of this invasion of my body then I had better arm myself with as much information as I could. I think that helped Jim too. He seemed to follow my lead and together we learned what we could do to deal with the cancer and get on with life.

Arrangements were quickly made so that at 9am the following day I would go into surgery and have the lump and surrounding tissue removed. My final question as I left the consulting room was: 'Can I still go to Antarctica?' I wasn't afraid of surgery, but I was terrified that I would lose the chance to achieve my goal. I only had two months before I was supposed to be sailing south and I needed to be told where I stood. The doctor assured me that if all went well I shouldn't have a problem.

All didn't go well. My surgeon, during the follow-up consultation, told me that extra growths had been discovered in the tissue he removed during the lumpectomy. After sinking back into my chair, absolutely stunned and horrified at what I had heard, I realised that to maximise my chance of getting to Antarctica I had to have a mastectomy as soon as a bed could be found at the hospital. It was clear-cut for me, I simply didn't have the time to consider any less radical treatment.

Walking out of the doctor's office after this latest blow was like moving around in someone else's dream. I couldn't believe that this was really happening to me. I felt surreal standing in the empty waiting room watching Jim at the little window paying the account after the consultation and collecting the necessary paperwork. Everyone in the cramped office was so polite and everything seemed so terribly normal. As I stood back looking at the scene I could feel a primal scream deep inside me that was trying to escape – I was terrified and wanted to wail to the world that I was about to lose my breast to cancer! Me – Yvonne Claypole!

Minutes passed like hours and I remember turning away towards the corner of the room and crying quietly, hoping that no one would notice. Jim did. He came over and held me tight. Vera, the secretary, just waited very quietly. I knew that she must have felt some of my pain too. I believe any woman would, along with a touch of guilt for the inevitable relief that it wasn't her. I know that Jim was aching deep down with sadness too and trying not to cry as he enclosed me in his arms. I felt safe and loved, and very glad that I didn't have to face this cancer monster on my own.

My focus to get to Antarctica never wavered. Once I was convinced that I wasn't about to die, the proportions of the threat began gradually to diminish. I knew that I was going to have to undergo a lot of changes in terms of my thinking about myself, particularly the acceptance that I wasn't immortal after all. And for me that was one hell of a shock! I would need time to recover from the second operation, as I knew that that was going to set me back a bit. Despite everything, I was convinced that having something as wonderful as fulfilling a dream meant that the news of my cancer couldn't take over my life. I had too many other good things to worry about and get on with.

Having Jim right beside me, I'm certain, was another important reason why I didn't just curl up in a ball and indulge in copious amounts of self-pity. It sounds corny but it's true – with him there I knew that I was always going to find a way to cope. We were spending all of our days together at that stage and we were able to talk whenever either of us had a need – if we were still out working at our separate jobs it would have been vastly different. Being able to confront our feelings together, on the spot, meant that the dimensions of the monster began to diminish.

Jim found the whole episode just as frightening and bewildering as I did, but he was always there for me. He didn't encroach on my thoughts and allowed me the space I needed to process everything that was going on in my life. He listened and talked as I wanted to. He was physically close and loving. Neither of us liked what was happening but we soon came to the realisation that we had to deal with it and move on or else the cancer was going to take over both our lives.

I was concerned, however, that my breast cancer might make me a liability in the eyes of some of our sponsors. Would they see me as a bit too much of a risk? I was to learn very quickly that, if anything, they were inspired by my decision to continue with my dream and they encouraged me further.

To me the loss of the breast itself wasn't a big issue. I made jokes about my impending lopsided shape but as the date for surgery drew nearer I found that I was looking more closely at myself in the mirror trying to imagine how my chest would look. I'd always been a bit light on in the girlie curves department – and so: 'Who'd notice anyway?' teased Vicky, my loving younger sister. I had frequent little weeps in private, not so much because I felt miserable but to relieve the inner tension that always seemed to be there.

There were lots of people I had to tell about my breast cancer, even though my initial response was to keep it fairly close and just to get on with it. I came to realise, however, that that was a selfish attitude and very unfair to the people who cared about me. I have always tended to shrug away offerings of kindness and help in the past, as I felt a bit uncomfortable with it. I have this rather arrogant attitude that I can do everything myself. I think it stems back to the days when Jim was in the Navy and I was left on my own for months or years at a time. I had a desperate need to prove to everyone, particularly myself, that I could manage on my own. This time I was out of my depth and I knew I would need help. My friends and family were genuinely shocked but incredibly sensitive in the way they responded to my news. I was very moved by their love and support and for once I didn't resist but let it wash over me and basked in its warmth.

The news was hard for my sons Ryan and Ben to accept. They both responded with a stunned silence. Perhaps like me they believed that life would always go on the way it had and that someone from our family couldn't be struck down in this way. They didn't ask a lot of questions or talk about it with me spontaneously, and I didn't know what was going through their minds. I probably fostered this initially by making light of everything and trying to act as if this were no more than a wart that needed to be removed. Consequently there were a lot of things they didn't properly understand about what was going on with my body. It took me a while to realise this and to get to them privately and individually and talk it out with them.

One very important group of people that I knew would be greatly worried by the news of my breast cancer were the students at school. *New Idea* and Channel 9's *A Current Affair* were both planning to release the expedition story including the discovery of my breast cancer. I didn't like the idea of my kids learning through the media that I had a life-threatening disease without being able to talk to me and see for themselves that I was really okay. Rhonda, the senior school coordinator, offered to break the news sensitively to all of the Grade 5/6 students, and I made arrangements to call into the school and talk with my own class.

I don't know who was the happier or more relieved to see the other, them or me. Gosh, I had missed them all! A sea of smiling faces surrounded me as I entered my old classroom for the first time in nearly two months. I immediately felt as if I had just returned home. All the smells, sounds and sights that had been a part of my day for the past 15 years were around me once again.

I sank down into my old overstuffed armchair that lived at the front of the room and two girls squeezed in beside me. After I'd heard all of the children's stories about what had been happening at school and home since I left in September, I brought them up to date on my expedition plans. They were a captive audience but still interested in everything to do with the adventure. They were very disappointed that I didn't have loads of gear yet to bring in to show them. Then I mentioned the discovery of my breast cancer and they all began to talk at once. Someone explained that Mrs Juniper had told them after sport on Friday and a lot of them had since talked among themselves and with their families as well. Each had some understanding of what was happening to my body, but their main concern was whether I could still go to Antarctica. I had to laugh because I thought they sounded just like me. And they were absolutely thrilled to hear that the trip was still on.

It had been arranged that the day before my surgery a film crew from *A Current Affair* would interview Jim and me at home. Initially

I'd felt horribly disappointed that our expedition hadn't generated much media interest until the discovery of my breast cancer, and I was very reluctant to be involved in the interview. Now, all of a sudden, a woman venturing down to the Antarctic to live in isolation with her husband after breast surgery seemed to capture everyone's imagination.

Although Jim and I had quickly learned to accept my breast cancer and weren't shy in talking about it with anyone, it wasn't meant to be the focus of our story. As far as I was concerned the work that we were doing for the Australian Museum, the Antarctic Division, the CSIRO, and Vic Ed with the international schools program was all far more newsworthy. I was reassured when told by the TV producer that the story would cover the entire expedition and that the recent discovery of my breast cancer would only be one small component. I agreed then to allow an interview the day before surgery, at the hospital and a week after surgery too.

The resulting story put to air about two weeks later was sensitively done and highlighted the fact that Jim and I were intent on following our dream together. This was the first time we had ever seen ourselves on telly and the camera certainly wasn't kind! I knew that I had been losing weight over the past months but I wasn't ready for what I saw. 'My God, I look so thin!' I exclaimed at the opening shot. 'I thought that TV was supposed to add kilos.' I decided there and then to bulk up my diet. I didn't want to go down south with no more fat on me than a knitting needle.

The response to our television story was extraordinary. Our phone ran hot for days! People whom we had not seen or heard from in years contacted us to pass on their heartfelt best wishes.

Ex-students from a long time past rang and promised to keep in touch with us over the following year. We were delighted with the strength of the positive response from everyone and warmed by their emotional support.

I woke up feeling well after surgery, a little sleepier than the last time, but not in any pain and I had no nausea, which is always a bonus after an anaesthetic. Jim and I couldn't wait to check out the wound. We couldn't see much, though, just the dressing that stretched from my breastbone to my armpit. I was shocked at how flat the area was. But I felt okay about it, even when I later had a more private inspection in the bathroom.

My doctor visited early the next morning and was pleased with what he saw. I was sitting crosslegged on the bed reading Sir Douglas Mawson's *The Home of the Blizzard* and tucking into a tub of yoghurt. Two hours later I was in our car, surrounded by all the lovely flowers and gifts that had arrived at the hospital. I was absolutely raring to get home and to get on with the expedition again, and I was enormously pleased with myself for being fit enough to leave hospital 24 hours after a mastectomy. Mind you, for the next three days I struggled to collect my thoughts coherently enough to have an intelligent conversation with anyone, let alone do much for myself. I decided that it must have been all that anaesthetic in my system.

The thought of returning to the doctor's rooms for the second post-surgery consultation filled me with dread. The last time I was there he hit me with the bombshell that the lumpectomy wasn't successful and that the cancer was not as small as expected. What would he tell me this time? Could anything else have been discovered that would again put an obstacle in the way of sailing to Antarctica in December?

But he was all smiles and encouragement, and said that he didn't want to see me again until I returned from the south in February 2000! We talked over what I could expect over the next twelve months in terms of my recovery and I was prescribed medication to help inhibit further breast cancers from growing. As I got up to leave he gave me a slip of paper with his e-mail address and phone number, and asked me to keep in touch with him. Yahoo – I was going to Antarctica, and thanks to modern technology I was now about to become one of the most remote patients in the world.

After receiving and following plenty of sound advice about nearly every aspect of our expedition, Jim and I finally had to confront the most difficult thing of all – the idea of writing up a disaster plan. Our geographic location at Cape Denison meant that for almost all of the year we could not be reached by the outside world. Jim and I accepted that once the crew of the yacht left us on the ice we were ultimately on our own. We were deeply excited by the necessity of total self-reliance and responsibility for our own survival. While that prospect thrilled us, we knew that it created a great deal of anxiety for others.

Our imminent adventure was ambitious and full of objective risks. Despite all the safety precautions we planned to implement it would have been stupid to say that nothing could go wrong. We were about to begin a journey on which there was a chance we might not return. Jim and I are firm believers that having great respect for the possibility of accidents raises your likelihood of survival. From the moment we set sail from Australia our safety was going to be challenged. In our minds the real nightmare for anyone back home would not be believing that something had gone horribly wrong for us but having to make a decision on what to do about it. We wanted to simplify all decision making in the event of our going missing, losing the means of communication or becoming ill or dying.

Jim and I spent a full day with my sister Vicky, her husband Steve, and Murray, detailing and documenting possible disasters, along with action plans and who we wanted to implement them. Together we identified a range of potential disasters that could occur from the moment we sailed into the Southern Ocean until the time we safely reached Australia again. These included perishing at sea and what we wanted done with our bodies if they were ever recovered.

Rescue from our part of Antarctica was impossible for most of the year, so we had to document what we would do if one of us became gravely ill or died, and how the news would be released at home. It is sobering to put down in black and white an agreement that in the event of the death of your partner you will place their body in a plastic bag and preserve it in the ice for the rest of the year. We also had to decide whether and how we wanted to be told if something happened to one of our family or close friends while we were away. There was even planning for the possible incidence of severe depression, and ways to support ourselves through it.

The final point stressed was that no rescue was to be called under any circumstances. Apart from the impossibility of reaching us for most of the time, we didn't want anyone putting themselves at risk in a rescue attempt. Our culture seems to hold the belief that life is not meant to be difficult, and that something or someone will always be there to catch those who fall. We were about to shatter that theory because on this venture it would be entirely up to us to do the catching.

Once the Dis-Plan document was complete we had to introduce it to our family. We called a family meeting, warning everyone that we would be presenting the plan in a businesslike manner for their information and input. We felt that it was far too emotive a topic to deal with in any other way. We all met in Ryan and Bronny's lovely new home one night and got straight into it.

What an amazing experience it was to sit with the people we loved most and talk with them about potential but very real disasters – our disasters. I was so proud of the way they listened, questioned and offered further ideas. We all talked it through objectively and in great detail. It was like preparing an insurance policy and it was treated with no more sentimentality than that. Everyone acknowledged that they understood and accepted our plan, then to my amazement they all went off together and had wine and nibbles in the kitchen. I was flabbergasted! I was expecting a more emotional response from everyone, especially me, and felt a twinge of hurt when it didn't emerge. Once I recovered from the shock I laughed at the absurdity of my feelings and joined the others.

Jim and I were comforted by the knowledge that our family had just confirmed their full acceptance of our adventure and our wishes concerning it. We knew that we were asking them for an enormous commitment to sharing our dream, even if it turned to tragedy. We realised how powerful an emotion love can be. Mum commented to us later that night that it was a terrific idea to have such a plan. She said that now she wouldn't worry because if anything went wrong it would be handled in exactly the way we wanted it to be. She said, as she hugged me tight: 'I think I can cope with that.'

Our dictionary's definition of adventure is 'participating in an exciting, possibly hazardous enterprise with an uncertain outcome'. Well, this trip to Antarctica certainly fitted that description. It was developing into the adventure of a lifetime.

4

Southern Ocean Sailing

During the preparation for Expedition Antarctica I learned that when planning something that big you need to be very flexible and prepared to change tack at any moment. Nothing is a given, as there are so many people, organisations, events and circumstances that can affect the outcome. Despite our great plans we never knew whether the expedition would succeed or not. So much was dependent on our preparation, our health, our gear and the condition of the ice as we ventured south. So I wasn't surprised or terribly perturbed when we heard in November that *Spirit of Sydney*, the yacht that was taking us down to Antarctica, had had an unexpected change of program.

Our departure date was originally set for around Christmas Day (1998), sailing from Bluff on the southern tip of New Zealand's South Island. *Spirit* was to arrive at Bluff from Tasmania via Macquarie Island with an Asian documentary film crew on board. A few days out from Hobart, in seas that weren't particularly rough, they lost the top section of the mast. The trip to Macquarie Island was abandoned and the yacht sailed back to Hobart and then on to Sydney under motor and a jury-rig for emergency repairs. With the necessity of replacing the entire mast, and such a tight time frame, it was decided that our departure point would change to Hobart and the date be set back a week to 6 January.

This was great news for Jim and me because it meant that we could have Christmas at home in Melbourne with our family. It also meant that Mum, Ryan, Ben, Bronny, Vicky and Steve could get down to Hobart to see us off. And transporting our equipment and food to Tassie for loading onto the yacht was going to mean less hassle and cost than flying it all across to Christchurch and trucking it down to Invercargill. The only downside to this unexpected change was that we lost 25 per cent of the cost of our airfares when we cancelled our prepaid tickets to New Zealand. Vicky agreed to follow up the refund, having bravely volunteered to take care of our personal financial details and mail while we were away.

Jim and I had never sailed before, so for us the outdoor part of this venture was to begin in earnest as soon as we stepped onto the yacht to head south. Jim had quite an advantage over me, though, as he had spent 20 years in the Royal Australian Navy. He hastened to make the point that sailing the oceans on a two and a half thousand tonne destroyer didn't quite compare with crossing the Southern Ocean in a 19 metre yacht. I agreed, but I thought Jim's advantage was still enormous. The closest I had ever come to travel on the water was paddling my touring kayak in the Murray River Marathon the summer before. Four days of flat-strap paddling in 40°C temperatures was no preparation for the sailing experience to come.

The first time we'd seen *Spirit of Sydney* was in August, when she was moored in a tiny cove on the north shore of Sydney. Don and

Margie had suggested that we go and have a look at the boat before driving back to Melbourne. We followed them down the jetty, gazing at the idyllic setting we were in. Steep cliffs surrounded the cove, with magnificent houses sprawled across them, all with enormous windows that faced across the water. It was drizzling lightly with rain and there wasn't another soul about.

Yachts of various sizes were anchored in the smooth grey waters of the bay, but none of them looked big enough to be *Spirit*. I looked over the few yachts tied up alongside the jetty but dismissed them without a second thought as there was obviously nothing large enough to sail to Antarctica and back.

I began to think we'd gone to the wrong marina and called out to Don: 'Where is she?' When he stopped suddenly and beamed down at a rather small, flat-looking yacht near the end of the jetty, I was horrified. 'My God! But it's so small!'

Don was obviously very proud of her and proceeded to apologise for the yacht not being at her best while having some maintenance work done. He and Margie gave us the grand tour, which didn't take very long. I felt pretty secure and comfortable wandering around, above and below deck – but then, we were tied to a jetty in a sheltered spot in the bay. I knew that the real test was going to be when we sailed out into the open sea and headed for the frozen south. The odd thing was, I really wanted to do that. If I were given the opportunity to fly to Cape Denison instead, I wouldn't take it. I would feel as if I was missing out on something really special, something a bit 'out there'. I decided that I wouldn't miss it for quids!

Jim and I were encouraged to make ourselves at home and even to try out the bunk for size. We were to occupy the 'honeymoon suite', one of the two double bunks on board. The skipper would have the other one opposite ours and next to the head (toilet). Our bunk was hardly queen-size, in fact when Jim lay on his back against the edge of the bed I was forced to lie on my side, or we wouldn't have fitted in. The crew had to make do with narrow bunks in tight places towards the front of the yacht. They shared their space with spare sails, lifejackets, ropes, harnesses, cans of food, pots and pans and their personal gear. Our little coffin-shaped bunk, with a parcel shelf to jam all our essentials onto, seemed positively luxurious in comparison.

The next time we saw *Spirit of Sydney* she looked magnificent. She was sporting a new mast and was tied up at the Royal Hobart Yacht Club along with many other boats, some much larger than she was. Our arrival in Hobart coincided with the late arrival of the last few yachts that limped in after the tragic 54th Sydney to Hobart Race. Of the 115 yachts that had begun the race, only 44 reached the finishing line at Constitution Dock in Hobart.

The mood was solemn as stories emerged about the horrific sailing conditions the fleet found themselves in when they tried to cross Bass Strait. Gusts of around 92 knots and huge waves claimed six lives and meant that a remarkable search and rescue operation had to be instigated. Fifty-five sailors were ultimately winched to safety; five boats sank. Memorial services were held for those who perished and a great feeling of sadness surrounded Hobart. Everyone was touched in some way by the tragedy.

Looking at the few broken and twisted yachts that had made it to Hobart, just remnants of what they had originally been, caused some of my anxieties about sailing to re-emerge. I knew that the stretch of water between Hobart and Antarctica could be dangerous for any vessel. Storms in excess of Force 12 and mountainous swells could be struck at any time. My mind began with the 'what ifs' again. I realised that I couldn't let myself become freaked out now. I was committed to this venture and that meant every part and component, even the sailing! I reminded myself that thousands of yachts cruise around the globe having a terrific time and we only hear of the disasters. *Spirit* had proven herself by sailing around the world once already and this was to be her sixth trip to Antarctica. She had more than adequately shown that she could deal with all that. I had to get on top of any fears and trust that the journey would be fine, then I could start to enjoy the experience – which was what the whole thing was about in the first place.

On 3 January we met Dave Pryce, the skipper, and the seven members of his crew. Although I had read a brief profile on each of them weeks before, it was lovely to put faces to names and to meet them all. I was completely taken aback at how young the skipper looked. The image I'd always held of seafaring captains was one of weathered features and grey hair. Dave was just a baby! At 27 he was the youngest on board, but by far the most experienced at extreme ocean sailing. This was to be his fifth trip down to Commonwealth Bay in *Spirit* and it became obvious that he was really looking forward to getting underway again.

For most of the crew this was to be their first Antarctic experience, and like us they were all on their own grand adventure. They had varying degrees of sailing experience from virtually none to a lifetime in the merchant navy. The crew hadn't sailed together until they joined the yacht on Boxing Day and began the Sydney to Hobart leg.

It was easy to see from all the friendly banter that despite the brief time together they had already established great rapport.

Last minute work on *Spirit* was being done and everyone was busy. Steve and Harry were compiling the final shopping list and asked if we wanted to make any additions. I jokingly asked if chocolate was included on the list. Dave, who turned out to be the biggest sweet tooth on board, broke into an enormous smile and said that there were two gigantic barrel loads already below. I couldn't think of anything else that I would want.

The final few days saw our gear disappear bit by bit into the confined spaces in the yacht. Goodness knows how it all fitted in, but Andy and Ian somehow found a place for everything. Our expensive and fragile communications equipment went onto the shelf over the foot of our bunk for safekeeping. That meant that there was barely any space for the small bag of clothing and personal items we were going to need on the trip down, but we managed to stuff it in. The little kangaroo emblem on the bow of the yacht disappeared up to its knees as *Spirit* sank lower in the water.

Media commitments punctuated our last days and nights. Television and radio stations from all over the country, as well as BBC London, wanted to talk with us before we left. Everyone was fascinated, and saw us as the 'couple from next door' who were about to spend twelve months alone together in one of the most inhospitable spots on earth. Jim and I both had mobile phones with us constantly so that we could take an interview anywhere, any time, and often at the same time too.

At last it looked as if we were ready. We were on the final countdown – only one more sleep to go. The chaos of last minute loading was over. I was standing with Jim at the Yacht Club rooms dreaming of a last cappuccino for twelve months and wondering if we could make time to escape into Hobart and indulge. We could hear Don joking with the crew, easing the tension. Our ears pricked up when we heard him announce: 'After the customs check tomorrow hand over your passports and I'll look after them until you get back.'

Passports!? Jim and I looked at each other wide-eyed, knowing that our passports were safely locked away at my sister's place in Melbourne, and she was here saying goodbye to us. 'Why do we need passports? We're going to Australian Antarctic Territory,' I stammered in disbelief. There was no arguing, though, we had to have them by morning or we couldn't leave Hobart. It was as simple as that.

Vicky offered to make an emergency dash to Melbourne, pick up the passports from her place and fly straight back to Tassie again. But it was peak holiday season and all flights were full. Her neighbour Fiona saved the day by using a spare key to enter Vicky's house and then sending the documents down by overnight courier. They would arrive on the first plane in the morning. 'What are we worried about? We'll have hours to spare!' Vicky joked.

By eight o'clock on the night before departure my emotions were in a fragile state and I was physically exhausted. Murray organised a large dinner at a restaurant in Hobart, though I wasn't keen to attend. I desperately wanted some time alone with my family but not in such a public place. Jim and I were the last to arrive at the restaurant, held up by a long final meeting with the McIntyres and the crew. I could barely eat anything and every time someone spoke to me I thought I'd cry. To my dismay everyone else had a hearty appetite and enjoyed themselves immensely. Shortly before midnight Jim and I escaped from the restaurant and crept back to the comfort and privacy of our hotel room.

In the morning helpful family members collected perishable food items ordered from Hobart shops by telephone weeks earlier. Now someone had to find space for 30 kilos of cheese, 40 kilos of Cryopac meat, 13 kilos of margarine and about 40 kilos of oranges, lemons, onions, potatoes, cabbages and bananas. Somehow everything disappeared below decks, most jammed into spaces between boxes and barrels. The meat was given priority one in the galley fridges.

We were set! I couldn't believe it, we had finally finished buying things. The weeks of 'shop till you drop' were over and we wouldn't have to enter a store again or open a wallet for more than a year. What's more, we had had our last shower and sat on our last flushing loo for the same period of time.

Everything was now on board but us. After a quick final customs clearance and telephone calls to our sponsors we would be on our way.

What do you say to your sons when you hug them for the last time for twelve months, maybe longer? We had already said our private goodbyes early in the morning before leaving the hotel, but now Jim and I were about to board the yacht. I wanted to say so much more to Ryan and Ben, to convey my love for them, to wish them safe and well, and to let them know they would always be with me.

All I could blurt out was: 'I love you ... look after each other.' I couldn't manage anything else as I thought I'd choke on the enormous lump in my throat. I knew that I wasn't doing a very good job at portraying a bold adventurer about to leave for the 'home of the blizzard'. I wondered if Mawson and his team had had this trouble. I hadn't counted on the farewell being so hard, as I had rehearsed it in my mind many times.

Motoring out of the marina in *Spirit*, I felt sure that everyone in the little group waving madly after us must have been glad to see us finally leaving. I was sure that after being caught up in the expedition whirlwind they were all saying: 'Just go!' I knew they were going to miss us, but at least now that we were on our way they could pick up the threads of their own lives again and catch up on some sleep. They all looked as exhausted as I felt. I fingered the tiny gold boomerang hanging from the gold chain around my neck and choked back tears as I thought of Vicky. She had given it to me at lunch the day before with the words: 'Boomerangs are meant to come back, you know. Stay safe.' Gosh, I was going to miss her. Vicky, my dearest and closest female friend, always provided unconditional love and sound advice when I most needed it. I hated the thought of being separated from her for so long.

My tears were soon replaced with feelings of sheer joy and excitement at beginning the adventure that Jim and I, and an incredibly supportive team of hardworking people, had been slogging towards for the last four months. I was still amazed that *Spirit* was going to sail all the way to Antarctica and even more amazed that we were going with her as the 'adventurers'.

We motored down the Derwent River for about an hour, then set the sails and raced along silently before the brisk wind. I sat in the cockpit surrounded by neat bundles of rope, all colour coded and attached to points on the sails and other places that I didn't even know about yet. The water rushed past us as we cut through the waves, and the water shooting out behind us was the only sound we could hear.

Our bare legs and feet basked in the warmth of the afternoon sun and I wondered how long it would be before we were forced to cover every part of our body with layers of thermals and protective Gore-Tex. The tops of the waves glistened where the sun penetrated them and the rest of the water around us sparkled and twinkled. The wind stiffened and the yacht heeled over quite steeply as we kept our course south. I surprised myself by not feeling alarmed as my toes pointed down towards the water. 'Maybe,' I thought, 'I could get to like this.' I wanted to shout out at the top of my voice: 'Hey, look everyone, I'm sailing!'

The Derwent River and the D'Entrecasteaux Channel, our route to the Southern Ocean, are huge. The scenery was spectacular as we sped past. My eyes were drawn to the mountain range silhouetted in the distance against a blue sky. Heavy white clouds sheathed the peaks and hid their craggy summits. Miniature houses were scattered across the steep green hillsides, all with superb views of the million-dollar setting.

The entire crew sat outside too, except Fitz who was navigator and working on the charts below. Everyone looked very relaxed and happy to be out on the water again. We all sat scrunched together in the cramped cockpit, chatting excitedly as only those who are about to launch into a shared adventure can. Talk centred on seasickness, how rough things might get, and us. Everyone had questions for Jim and me, although most tried not to be too obtrusive. We were honest and open in our replies. I think that everyone felt satisfied with them and we were made to feel welcome.

Time took on a new dimension as we easily slipped into the routine of four hours on watch and eight hours off. I caught up on some much needed sleep while Jim was on watch during the first few days at sea. When I wasn't on the bunk I was on the deck watching everything that was happening. I tried to stay out of everyone's way but it wasn't that easy. I was either blocking the helmsman's view of the navigational gauges, sitting on a rope that was being winched, or otherwise displaying a knack for being in the wrong place at the wrong time.

Sharing the trip with six other Antarctic first-timers was a buzz. Dave and Steve had been to the continent before but they were just as enthusiastic as the rest of us. Everyone was determined to enjoy everything about the trip and nothing went unnoticed or unphotographed. As we headed south on the momentum of the huge swells we all snapped the spectacular flight of the wandering albatrosses and then a pod of pilot whales breaching off the starboard bow. John's antics as he bathed off the back of the yacht in an icy two metre swell with nothing on but a harness and a smile were caught on film too.

Our journey southward offered everything we had hoped for: dolphins, seals, whales, extraordinary birdlife ... and no seasickness. Expecting that a landlubber like me would suffer from the dreaded seasickness I'd begun taking pills before sailing out of Hobart. I put great faith in those tablets to keep me feeling settled during the trip. I didn't care if it was really only mind over matter, as long as it worked. Jim, being an old sailor, thought that he wouldn't need them, despite the fact that it had been 15 years since he was last on a ship at sea. The closest I came to an upset stomach on the journey south was after eating a king-size chocolate bar in choppy seas. I felt a bit green around the gills even before I had stuffed the wrapper into my pocket and had to lie down for a while, vowing that I would never eat another chocolate bar again.

For the first few days out of Tassie, while the fresh food supplies were abundant, we ate like royalty. Steve produced bowls of fresh grapes, pineapple and oranges, followed by pancakes and plunger coffee, for breakfast on the first morning. I was so impressed with the guys who were obviously in their element in the galley. They even provided 'room service' – that is, they delivered meals to our bunks because there was no dining table on board and we had to sit on our beds to eat out of everyone's way.

Once the last of the fresh food was eaten, and the seas became increasingly rough, so did the standard of the meals. No one ever complained, though, particularly as we all had to take our turn in the galley. As long as it was hot and there was plenty of it we were all satisfied. It wasn't easy feeding ten hungry sailors with the yacht pitching and rolling with every wave. Often the bowls and plates would scoot off the benches before we could dish any of the meal up. On a few occasions cooking was banned as the conditions were too rough and dangerous, so dry crackers and anything that could be found to put on them were the go. Some chose not to eat at all on those days.

Once we crossed the Antarctic Convergence, which is where the warm water meets the colder water from the south, I started a 'book'. Estimations were recorded for the time and date of our crossing the Antarctic Circle, sighting the first iceberg and arriving in Commonwealth Bay. I really had no idea when any of those events was likely to take place but neither did any of the others, except Dave of course, and he wasn't allowed to give his estimations until the rest of us had locked ours in. This was also the day when John discovered that he'd left his toothbrush in Hobart. Someone offered him a spare but John said: 'I don't know whether I should brush my teeth or shave them.'

On Day Ten we were passing through another big low-pressure system. That always resulted in huge swells, and conditions for the blokes on watch became almost unbearably cold and wet. Flurries of hard-driven snow began to sting the unprotected parts of faces and everyone took more time and care in preparing to go on watch. The ocean temperature had been dropping rapidly and the salt spray blowing over the bow as we ploughed through the waves froze instantly on the rigging. Ice was forming on everything and everyone on deck.

Life below wasn't that much more pleasant. Everything below deck was wet thanks to the condensation dripping off the roof, leaks in the skylights, moisture from wet boots and foul weather gear, the rain and snow that had blown in, or waves that had washed inside. Fortunately, cold wet sleeping bags become snugly warm after you've been in them for a while – they just feel dank and horrible to get into.

Watching the sea form towering green walls around us made me uncomfortable. I felt very vulnerable to the whims of the sea, even though I was convinced by then that *Spirit* was a safe little vessel and had happily taken everything thrown at her so far. Nonetheless, I was happier below decks and not looking out in those conditions. A touch of the ostrich theory – if you can't see it, it's not there.

John suddenly called out from the deck: 'Iceberg!' Skipper Dave raced outside, anxious to get a quick bearing on the ice as we approached it. John then chuckled behind his frozen balaclava as he showed Dave the 'nice bird' flying by.

During Jim's afternoon watch, which he shared with Guy and Harry, the first real iceberg was sighted. Not a 'nice bird' this time. Harry won the KitKat for predicting the time and date most closely. Guy had spotted the berg way off on the horizon, a large ghostly shape, barely discernible in the poor visibility.

Everyone crowded on deck, pulling on their hats and gloves and foul weather jackets, to see the enormous white monolith as it got nearer. For most of us this was our first real taste of Antarctica and we were astonished to find the berg towering way above our mast. We guessed that it was about the height of a five storey building. As we approached the icy monster, another even larger one was sighted on the port side of the yacht. Our camera shutters were working wildly as we all recorded the awesome experience of sailing silently and gracefully between two great mountains of floating ice.

We sailed past multitudes of bergs, the variety of sizes and shapes defying description. Some were the size of small islands, while others were weird and grotesque shapes. All were slowly dissolving as the massive waves ate away at their base. The rays of the sun picked out prominent features of each berg and made them glisten as they rose and sank in the icy swell.

I was so overcome with emotion watching them looming out of the mist around us that I felt choked up and could barely speak. No book, film or photo had prepared me for such magnificence. It was beyond beauty.

Forgetting all about my sailing anxieties I perched close to the railing, swaying back and forth with the swell, feet freezing in my rubber sailing boots, ears and cheeks tingling in the cold. I was unable to comprehend that I was actually a part of this extraordinary setting and not just watching another documentary. I hugged myself excitedly when Dave announced that we had only 281 nautical miles to go before arriving at Cape Denison, the climax of our journey.

The radar screen was switched on and monitored by Dave and Jerry for the next two days. It was important to keep scanning for any big bergs in our path. Everyone else settled down with the realisation that we had arrived at the more serious end of the trip. Dave reminded us that we all needed to keep our wits about us and to be on the alert 24 hours a day for ice in the water.

The big bergs weren't going to be much of a problem for us as we could see them easily a long way off and change our course as needed. It was the bergy bits that were going to be our main hazard. These are the chunks of broken-up bergs that can be as small as an Esky or the size of a car. They roll backwards and forwards on the waves and can't be seen until they are right on you. Dave said: 'If we hit one at speed it'll put a hole in *Spirit* and we'll all be in deep shit.' I was reminded of something I had read that said human survival in the minus 2°C waters of the Southern Ocean could be measured in minutes. The tongue in cheek advice of the author was that since drowning was far preferable to freezing to death, anyone that found themself overboard was to swim as hard as they could for the bottom.

The term 'keeping watch' had a whole new meaning for us. While one crew member on duty manned the wheel, the other two were close to the bow trying to discern the foam of waves breaking on icebergs. The conditions were appalling and the two hour watches must have seemed like an eternity, something that had to be endured.

The air temperature had begun to drop well below zero and the water that was dumping on us with each wave was a couple of degrees below. It was just as well that the nights were as bright as day by then, as it would have been positively scary sailing among the ice in the dark. The mood was very tense but at the same time everyone seemed exhilarated. This was what we were there for, to be part of an Antarctic experience, and we were getting our share of it.

We were rapidly approaching the coast of the continent, which meant that our crossing of the notorious Southern Ocean was almost completed. I couldn't help but feel that we had been let off lightly this time, having pounded through the Roaring Forties, Furious Fifties and Screaming Sixties. My emotions were in turmoil. I felt thrilled and enormously relieved that we had survived what I considered to be one of the most hazardous parts of the venture, but I was also fully aware that we weren't safely on land yet. There were no guarantees that conditions in Commonwealth Bay were going to allow us to approach the coast, let alone motor into Boat Harbour and moor safely. We were going to be completely at the mercy of the treacherous katabatic winds that roared down from the polar ice cap. There was no way we could sail or motor against such a force once the winds started up, and we would have to head out to sea again until they dissipated. The latest radio weather report from the meteorologist at Australia's Casey Base indicated that the katabatics were blowing between midnight and 1pm each day, and that the sea ice in that area was open. Dave grinned at me, so I felt quietly confident that we were going to make it.

I wondered how Jim was feeling at the time. Did he have any apprehensions about what lay ahead of us? I glanced across at him as he stood at the helm listening intently for each shout from the bow, ready to respond instantly to avoid colliding with the unseen chunks of ice. His concentration was intense so I decided that he probably wasn't contemplating the future right now. I watched him quietly working away at the wheel and was reminded of how much I loved him.

A huge part of my joy at living out this amazing dream was having Jim right there beside me. I wouldn't have wanted to do this without him. We were headed for one of the most beautiful but inhospitable spots on Earth, where the isolation meant that we were directly responsible for our own survival. I was stoked that I was going to have Jim all to myself for a year and was eagerly looking forward to waving the crew goodbye and beginning our time alone.

5.

Bums on the Ice

Walk quietly in any direction and taste the freedom of Antarctica.

Colin Monteath

The wind quietened down suddenly and the seas began to flatten. I was feeling disappointed that we had missed the experience of sailing through some pack ice, although I felt sure that Dave was relieved to find that the strong winds had broken it up a week before and blown the ice far out to sea. I had often imagined motoring gently through the smooth ice in a dead calm sea watching penguins and seals at play or basking in the Antarctic sun. The reality is that Commonwealth Bay is rarely so idyllic. Antarctica calls the shots, and I had to learn to expect the unexpected.

On Sunday 17 January 1999, eleven days after leaving the Derwent River, we had our first sighting of Antarctica. It was like an apparition. I thought I was looking at a massive cloudbank behind some closer bergs. I wasn't prepared for the reality of the enormous ice slope that rose so high out of the sea. It looked so vast and so white! It was a landscape purely of snow, ice and sky. I looked around and tried to take in the scenery, noting the stunning light and crystal atmosphere of the place.

As we edged closer I gazed mesmerised by the towering ice cliffs that shaped the coastline. They must have stood a hundred or more metres above the waves crashing against their base. Beyond were massive fields of crevasses, bigger and bluer than I had seen anywhere before. We couldn't sail too close, as they were the calving grounds for icebergs that have been breaking off the massive glaciers for thousands of years. As beautiful and benign as they looked, a sudden collapse of the ice edge and tonnes of ice would crash into the water, creating waves that could swamp our tiny vessel.

I now noticed a rocky point jutting out in the distance. 'My God, look! There's Cape Denison!' I yelled, pointing to the dark speck about ten kilometres away. This was the only accessible area of rock for hundreds of kilometres along the Antarctic coast.

Most of the rock on Cape Denison, according to Mawson, is 'a uniform type of gneiss crumpled and folded, showing signs of great antiquity'. There is no soil or gravel on the Cape, just rocks and ice, as any light materials are blown away by the winds. Cape Denison's climate is severe. Prolonged blizzards are common. The fierce winds that batter the Cape all year long drain the cold air off the enormous ice cap to the south.

The coast of Antarctica is subject to two kinds of winds: those that result from the low-pressure areas circling the Southern Ocean; and the mighty katabatic winds that originate inland and take the form of dense, cold air pouring down from the plateau. At Cape

Denison the strength of a katabatic wind is dramatically increased by the funnelling effect as it passes through the valleys towards the coast. Katabatics can also produce phenomena such as revolving whirlpools of cloud and walls of drifting snow. The winds may surge suddenly to high speeds and then stop in an instant. Both types of wind were a significant threat to us and would largely determine whether we could sail into Boat Harbour that day. Dave was watching the weather indicators carefully.

It seemed that Antarctica was breaking with tradition and had decided not to send down the inland winds that she had been dispatching regularly at 1pm. It was bloody cold, though, and still too windy to allow *Spirit* to safely enter Boat Harbour. By late evening we sailed as close to the Cape as was considered safe and temporarily anchored in the lee of the massive cliffs to the west of the harbour. Guy, Andrew and Ian prepared the inflatable dinghy ready to putt-putt around the rocky spit and enter the harbour. They received last minute instructions from Dave on how to set the mooring lines and stern warnings of the dangers of collapsing ice ledges still surrounding the harbour.

It was tough going for the little craft. There was enough wind gusting to whip the waves into quite a chop and on a couple of occasions it threatened to flip the dinghy over. The outboard motor was barely able to make headway. Twice the engine cut out. Guy reacted quickly and threw the drogue out to act as a sea anchor to slow the boat down, but the tiny inflatable was blown out towards the rocks at an alarming speed. We all watched tensely from the deck of the yacht. Dave began singing quietly to himself – always a giveaway sign that he was extremely anxious – as he watched Guy restart the motor and begin to head back towards the harbour. I guess Dave knew better than anyone did the disastrous scene that may have been unfolding before our eyes. The dinghy fought hard against the turbid water around the rocks and made for the harbour entrance.

Suddenly the wind dropped slightly and the choppy waters quietened. Dave sprang into action. We motored into the harbour, taking advantage of the calm spell, fully aware that it might only be momentary. We were all tense as we rounded into the harbour. Small and compact, Boat Harbour is a tiny inlet shaped like a boot almost completely landlocked. It is big enough to hold only one yacht snugly between its overhanging ice ledges and rough rocky shores. We were to anchor and tie up right in the centre of the harbour, the only place deep enough to safely moor.

Dave was in control of *Spirit*, taking charge of the wheel and the throttle. The entrance to Boat Harbour is narrow and shallow, skirted by clearly visible or roughly charted rocks and ice ledges. The approach is crucial. With the bow pointing straight down the length of the little harbour we made easy headway to the point where Dave wanted to drop anchor. All of a sudden the mood on board relaxed as we realised where we were. We'd made it! I threw my arms around Jim and he hugged me tight. 'We're home,' he exclaimed, grinning broadly.

Dave wasn't celebrating yet, as he knew we were still in an extremely vulnerable position sitting in the shallow waters without any secure lines ashore. The wind was likely to scream down off the ice cap without warning and we wouldn't have a chance of preventing *Spirit* from smashing against the rocks. The consequences wouldn't bear thinking about.

While the crew was at work setting the first mooring lines I took the chance to get out of everyone's way, look around and soak up the spectacle surrounding me. The sounds of the winches, chains and shouting voices faded as I looked beyond *Spirit*'s deck and marvelled at the frozen world. All exposed rocky mounds were dotted with thousands of nesting Adelie penguins. The rocks were pale brown, covered with unknown generations of penguin poo, and the smell, even from my position out on the yacht, was overpowering. Don had once described it as a chookpen smell, and I thought that came pretty close.

At the end of the harbour, nestled into the icy slope, was Mawson's Hut. I felt a rush of emotion as I made out the two roofs – the original battered brown roof of the main hut, and the stark new orange one that covered the derelict roof of the smaller workshop in front. Everything was just as I had seen in the old black and white photos taken by Frank Hurley during the 1911–1914 Australian Antarctic Expedition. Apart from the sporty new roof nothing appeared to have changed. I half expected to see Mawson and some of his men come out of the hut and make their way down to the water's edge to welcome us to Cape Denison.

Behind the hut is a gradual snow slope, and beyond that a dark crescent of glacial moraine, like a dirty streak on the steep ice slope. I knew that a vast, featureless nothing lay beyond my sight, leading all the way across the polar ice cap. Even great deserts are not as barren as the two and a half thousand kilometres of frozen terrain that separated us from the Amundsen–Scott Base at the South Pole.

The landscape to the west of us was dominated by the highest rocky point on the Cape, which proudly held the imposing wooden cross erected 86 years ago in memory of Xavier Mertz and Belgrave Ninnis, who were Mawson's two companions during an exploratory sledging journey far to the east of Cape Denison. Ninnis disappeared down a bottomless crevasse, along with his sled and dogs. Mawson and Mertz were left with little food, no tent and six starving dogs. They were forced to eat their huskies to survive. Mertz sickened and died, poisoned by the dog livers he'd eaten. Mawson struggled alone for the final 160 kilometres back to Cape Denison, enduring appalling cold, white-outs and starvation. He arrived back at the hut only to see his ship sailing out of the harbour returning to Australia. Mawson was forced to spend a second year in Antarctica before he could be rescued. I thought of the epic sledging trip on which the two young lives were tragically lost and was awestruck to be in the location where they spent their winter preparing for that journey. I remembered reading somewhere that each bit of wood used to make the memorial cross was a slat from the bunks of the dead men. I made a mental note to look for those two incomplete bunks when I entered Mawson's Hut.

Jim stood beside me and gazed silently about. 'What do you think?' he asked. 'It's just like the photos,' I said. 'I feel like I've been here before.' For months we had pored over any photographs and maps of the area that we could get our hands on, and everything now felt strangely familiar to me. The reality of being there evoked far more of an emotional response than any images we had seen before. I couldn't get the smile off my face.

Jim began pointing out prominent landscape features such as Penguin Knob, the Mackellar Islands and Proclamation Hill. Although we couldn't see Gadget Hut from our present position we had a fair idea where it was and I picked out the snow ridge we would walk over to get there … assuming it was still there! No one had seen it since last summer when a working party was on the Cape continuing with the restoration of Mawson's Hut.

In this environment it was easy to imagine a tiny structure like Gadget Hut being literally blown away in a blizzard and disappearing into Commonwealth Bay. Jim and I had already discussed the possibility of arriving on the Cape and discovering that the hut had been destroyed. We knew that if the damage was extreme, and we were unable to repair it with the limited resources and time we had available, then we would have no other choice than to return with the yacht. Survival in Antarctica is impossible without shelter. To have achieved so much of our dream, only to be forced to turn back, would have been soul destroying for Jim and me and a great many other people too. We were very keen to get ashore and reassure ourselves that our little home was safe and sound.

Such a magical Antarctic scene couldn't be marred, even by the sight of nearby Granholm Hut and the sprawling mess around it. The hut is an ugly old ANARE (Australian National Antarctic Research Expedition) emergency shelter, constructed around 1978. About 20 metres from the hut are two large, rusty old seatainers and a number of equally rusty 44 gallon drums strewn among the rocks and very close to a nearby rookery. I knew that there were plans to remove the dreadful eyesore, leaving the historical site free from such intrusions. I hoped that it would be done soon and the integrity of the heritage area restored. I turned away and watched a group of Adelies porpoise their way through the water beside the yacht.

I was snapped back to reality by the crackling static of the VHF radio. Andrew was reporting from shore and told Dave that the mooring lines stored under Granholm Hut were solidly iced in and that despite their efforts with ice axes they could not remove them. The bulky ropes were lying beneath the hut, placed there by the crew of *Spirit of Sydney* when they were last in Commonwealth Bay two years before. The rocks formed a natural bowl shape and had filled with meltwater at some stage. The rope had been completely submerged in the water before it froze solid again. The hut floor was only centimetres above the large iceblock with the mooring lines trapped inside, which meant that there was virtually no room to wield an axe in an attempt to release them.

Five hours, seven men with assorted picks and shovels, and two pots of boiling water later and nearly everyone was ready to accept that the ropes had become a permanent fixture in Antarctica's ice. Seven frozen, hungry and almost exhausted men returned to the yacht while the midnight sun continued to blaze. We all ate a hot and hearty 'hoosh' (leftover casserole with a couple of cans of baked beans thrown in) at 1:30am, our body clocks askew already.

Dave issued directions for setting extra mooring lines for the night. They were not as strong as the ones ashore, but they eased Dave's mind by increasing our safety margin somewhat. The katabatic wind was still to hit us and we knew that when it did every line and anchor point would be strained to the limit. Frozen to the bone and so tired that we were barely able to function we all collapsed into our bunks at 5:15am. We were totally unaware of any wind that may have roared down upon us that night. We slept like babies.

A motley, dishevelled crew assembled around the navigation table at mid-afternoon the following day. No one had been out of their bunk for long, so food and drink was everyone's priority. We all munched on canned fruit and custard while Dave laid out the plans for the day. A group of four men were to spend the entire day if necessary chipping the lines out of the ice beneath Granholm Hut. Dave made it clear that they *must* be freed and *Spirit* moored securely even if it took 24 hours to achieve. He emphasised that the men had to work as if their lives depended on it. 'Because they may well do, if a hundred knot wind gets up,' he said.

Another party was to assist Jim and me in the task of unloading our tonnes of gear. We had to take full advantage of the calmer weather and try to ferry everything from the yacht to establish a cache in the relative protection of the rocks on the eastern side of the harbour. We were told to always be ready for the weather to change for the worse and to work like mad to accomplish what we could before that happened. Once a blizzard set in we could be confined to the yacht for days.

We began organising ourselves to go ashore, which was some feat. By the time we had put on full Antarctic gear – boots, thermals, windstopper jacket, neck warmer, hat, Gore-Tex salopettes (bib and brace overalls) and jacket, along with gloves and goggles – it was hard to see where we were going, let alone move there. I took on the proportions and grace of a Sumo wrestler as I readied myself to clamber off the back of the yacht into the iced-up inflatable dinghy bobbing at the stern.

Jim descended into the dinghy first to chip off the ice sheathing and to move a crate of gear to make room for the passengers. His boots broke through the ice layer in the bottom of the boat and sank into centimetres of near frozen water. He yelled for something to bail with. Despite all his frantic bailing with the ice cream container someone threw to him the water level didn't drop. When he saw a small rubber object floating around the bottom of the boat and held it up to see if anyone knew what it was, the look on his face was priceless when Guy shouted back: 'The bung! It's the bung!' We all nearly died laughing at Jim scrambling across the bottom of the dinghy looking for the drainage hole to stick it in before the boat sank any further.

It was a beautiful sunny Antarctic day as we readied to motor ashore, with a cold 20 knot breeze blowing to ensure that we didn't forget where we were. The air temperature was only minus 4°C, mild by local standards, but the wind chill factor made it a very cold minus 21°C – cold enough to frost-nip any unprotected fingers and cheeks. I adjusted my clothing and climbed into the dinghy. Jim and I were in the first group off the yacht.

Waterproof gloves were put to the test as everyone on board the rubber inflatable flexed their muscles and hauled the boat hand-over-hand along one of the mooring lines. Rather than start up the motor we crawled silently along the icy water to the eastern edge of the harbour. Dave had selected that spot as possibly the safest and most accessible at that time for offloading our gear. Luckily we all kept our sea boots on because each of us plunged into the water as we slipped and slid off the smooth icy rocks along the water's edge.

The arrival of our grey dinghy didn't impress one of the locals. We all jumped back when a massive 400 kilogram Wedell seal sunning himself on a rock nearby lunged at the side of the boat, apparently intent in ripping a hole in it. Wedells are renowned for their beautifully placid nature, so this attack was totally unexpected. Guy responded by yelling a few choice words and the seal seemed to get the message. He haughtily slithered out into deeper water and let us be. In contrast, the friendly Adelie penguins were extremely excited by our presence and crowded and jostled close by, squawking and flapping their flippers at everything we did.

While the guys began offloading some small gear we headed up over the ridge for our first look at Gadget Hut together. As we crested the icy slope, suddenly there it was, snugly nestled between two rocky outcrops and with a halo of snow around three sides. It looked so small and cute sitting there by itself surrounded by a vast nothingness that my heart did a little flip. I knew that we were in Antarctica to stay, now that I had seen Gadget Hut, and I couldn't wait to throw open the door and look inside.

In my eagerness I began running down the slope. Although I had chains on my boots for added traction, the surface was too slick and I scooted on my bottom down to the rocky gully beside the hut. Laughing, I called back to Jim to hurry up, and we arrived at the door together.

We both hesitated, spontaneously. I don't know what was going through Jim's mind but I was relishing the moment. I was thinking that the instant we stepped into the hut we were leaving behind all the uncertainties that had plagued us over the past months. Our planning was over, the Southern Ocean had allowed us safe passage, and we had arrived on the continent with all our gear intact. And now we knew that Gadget Hut was still standing and ready to shelter and protect us. We had taken on so many risks to fulfil our dream, and at this moment it had proved all worthwhile.

Neither of us spoke as Jim reached up and released the locking handles – no padlocks required here, not too many crooks find their way to Cape Denison. My mind was racing as I wondered whether I would find the place intolerably small. Would I feel claustrophobic anxiety when shut up inside? I heard Don's reassuring words again: 'Don't worry if the place looks really small and cramped when you first go in. After a while it seems to grow bigger.'

The small front door entered directly into an annex, which was a wooden lean-to attached to the northern end of the hut. It was obvious that this was a great place for storage and it was crowded with heaps of gear left behind by the McIntyres. We squeezed in so that we could shut the door behind us.

The first thing that struck me was the smell. I had never come across anything like it before. I can only describe it as a chemically/fuelly kind of smell. Eventually we were to become used to it, as it permeated everything that we ever brought into the hut, including us. We called it the 'Gadget smell' and used to laugh when everyone at home was bowled over by it when we began unpacking after our return.

There wasn't much headroom in the annex as the roof sloped at a very sharp 45 degree angle, so I was eager to move into the living area. Opening the interior door revealed an incredibly cramped space that was originally designed as an airlock to keep the foul weather out of the living quarters. This space was only 90 centimetres wide and only one of us could step into it at a time. Still not saying anything, I held my breath and opened the final door. 'Oh my God, it's huge,' I teased Jim. 'Look, standing room for four!'

Jim bundled in beside me and we stood and stared. What a lovely, long awaited sight! The three miniature windows allowed enough Antarctic night sun to pour into the room so that we could see everything quite clearly, not that there was really much to see. If I'd had to come up with a word on the spot to describe the inside of the hut it would be 'basic'.

Directly opposite the door were the table and two bench seats with packing cases behind that served as shelves. The bed platform was above this and it looked confined and dark up there. I noticed that there wasn't a ladder to climb up, so I guessed that the table would come in handy to help me hurl myself up. On our right was the kerosene stove. The sink, with no plumbing attached, sat on more open packing cases. There was a 25 litre plastic water barrel on the shelf above them.

The kitchen bench was on our left, with more wooden crates beneath for storage of food. I noticed the microwave oven sitting on a shelf above the bench and was sorry that we weren't able to use it for anything but storing crockery. It was a white elephant because we simply couldn't spare enough power to run it. A small kerosene heater stood on the floor by our feet. And that was it – home for the next twelve months. I gave Jim an excited hug and said: 'Let's move in, then.'

At the yacht, Ian and Andrew began to pull our precious cargo out of the hold and on to the deck, ready to be passed to Gerry and Guy who were waiting alongside in the inflatable. Once the boxes were ferried carefully to the water's edge Jim, Harry and I carried them up over the ice ledges and stacked them safely in the rocks nearby.

All our food supplies and a lot of other equipment were packed into cartons that had been lined with plastic. Each box was then double wrapped in heavier-grade plastic and securely taped and boldly numbered. Ravi from Amcor Containers had worked with us back in November to find the best way to keep salt water, ice and snow from affecting the quality of our food and gear throughout the expedition, and the result was excellent. At no time during the year did the packaging let us down.

There was also an assortment of odd sized and shaped packages, plus screwtop barrels containing our climbing gear, and the wooden panels for the prefabricated aerial housing. When the panels were ferried from the boat I stood precariously on the icy rocks and reached out to receive them. Gerry yelled out, 'Watch the wind!', as I held the boards at arm's length in front of me. Too late ... within a fraction of a second a wind gust caught the largest piece broadside and smashed it back into my face. Everyone heard the loud crack of my nose being whacked, and saw me go down. At least there was plenty of ice to apply to my rapidly swelling schnozz. After I'd recovered from the shock I felt pretty sure it wasn't broken, but I knew that I would be sporting a couple of beautiful black eyes by morning.

Hour after hour of hard work meant that we worked up quite a sweat. Sometimes I would remove my gloves without thinking, only to be snap-frozen. Then I would have to stamp around shaking my hands to warm them up again inside my gloves.

By midnight we had finished unloading *Spirit*. Standing on the rocks by the shore we were surrounded by piles of everything we were going to need for the year – food, safety equipment and communications gear. We also had crate loads of books, music and hobby items. Just as well we planned to be busy with other projects, because suddenly the things didn't look as though they were going to last us long. Jim and I hoped that we hadn't been too ruthless in trimming down our entertainment supplies.

We all returned on board to a magnificent roast dinner, which we ate hungrily – chocolate bars and bottled water were all we'd had since breakfast. Without exception everyone looked weary. Even John couldn't find the energy to crack a joke or tell a funny story. But Dave had more in store for us. 'The mooring lines under Granholm aren't yet free,' he said, 'and the Claypoles' boxes need to be sledded the 400 metres to their hut. So while the weather's still relatively calm we'll all head out again after dinner and meet back at the launching spot at 4am.'

Stepping back outside into the bright night we spotted John and Ian struggling over the crest of the ridge pulling a heavily laden sled behind them with the first of the boxes for our new home. Between the four of us we managed to haul quite a few loads to the hut before the 4am curfew. This was to be our last night on *Spirit*.

The next eight days were wonderful. While Dave and the crew busied themselves with various things Jim and I moved into our shoebox home, leaving everything but the essentials stacked on the ice outside. At around 1:30pm on the first day in the hut we heard the katabatic wind start. The suddenness and the strength of the initial blast shocked us. Great clouds of fine drift hurtled down from the ice slopes behind us and blasted the walls of the hut, then blew out and dissipated over Commonwealth Bay. I hoped that the crew who were ashore managed to motor back to the yacht safely, otherwise they'd have to spend the night in here with us. And that would be cosy!

As the wind gained in strength I worried about our boxes sitting out on the ice. They were very exposed out there and if we didn't secure them they might be blown away and end up in the penguin rookery below us. We grabbed our foul weather jackets, some snowstakes and ropes and plunged outside to lash the boxes down.

Lesson one: *Always* take the time to dress appropriately before going outside. That means covering *all* parts of the body with full protective gear.

Jim and I felt the full force of the icy gale on those parts of our body not fully protected. We were outside for only ten minutes or so but we were absolutely frozen when we escaped back inside again. We felt very sorry for ourselves when the sharp burning sensations began as the various body parts warmed up. Never again!

A lot of the McIntyres' gear, which was mainly emergency supplies, had to be moved out and stored somewhere so that we could begin to bring in our own stuff. We sledded most of it across to Jubilee Base, the second Antarctic Division hut about a kilometre away. Halfway up the first hill, with a sled-load dragging behind me, my leg muscles began to scream. Boy, was my fitness in a shocking state! I wanted to take my hat off or loosen my collar and jacket as I had already begun to overheat, but as soon as I did the cold was excruciating. I knew that I had to ease off in order to cool down and avoid sweating. It was slow hard work but we were in need of the exercise after the confinement of the yacht, and we didn't mind because we now had the chance to see some of the most spectacular views on the Cape.

Antarctic snow has its own character. It is dry and grainlike, with the appearance and texture of sand. It is fused together by the cold and can become very hard. The colour is stunning in that it's the whitest of whites imaginable. And we found that we had trouble getting a shovel into it. It was like striking rock. We soon discovered that it was easier to cut blocks rather than dig out shovel-loads, and that's how we constructed an ice cave to store our precious supply of cryovacced meat.

The curved pruning saw, taken specifically for that task, cut through the compacted snow easily and we used an ice axe to prise the blocks clear to create a deep cave. We then used the blocks to construct an ice wall along the front. Thoroughly enjoying the 'Eskimo experience', we got a little carried away with our igloo building and made it far bigger than necessary. When Jim crawled in and was able to lie down I decided we had made it big enough! A wooden board formed a door to close over the opening, and the spot was marked with a snowstake in case it disappeared during a snowstorm.

Before removing our meat from the temporary ice trench we had first dug beside the hut we popped a thermometer deep inside the cave for 24 hours to check the internal temperature. At that time, early in the year, it was around minus 7°C and we knew that it was going to get much colder. We were also satisfied that our meat would be safe from the skuas that had been lurking close by looking for a change in their penguin diet. It was just as well that I kept an inventory of the contents because the cave always filled up with drift and I was constantly losing little plastic packages of meat. I also placed Mum's Christmas cake in the cave, wedging it in securely at the far end between the bacon and the roast beef. It would be a long time before we saw it again.

Whenever the katabatics raged we used the time to work inside. While I unpacked and tried to find places to store our stuff Jim tackled the electrical system with enthusiasm. He had to connect the two solar panels to the three marine dry cell batteries that were to store our power. An inverter was also connected to the system to convert the 12 volt output to 240 volts for our few electrical appliances. He also checked over the 4hp diesel generator that we would use during winter when there was no sunlight on the solar panels. After an oil change it started easily and Jim ticked it off his checklist.

Quickly establishing communications with the outside world was a high priority. We desperately wanted to tell everyone at home that we had our bums on the ice and that they could start cracking the champagne bottles we'd left with them to celebrate the occasion. We had two satellite telephones, a Sat M which could provide basic telephone facilities and was to be our standby phone, and a super-duper expensive Sat B phone which would allow us to send voice, data, digital images and video.

We tried ringing Ryan's place on Sunday afternoon on the Sat M. I could barely contain my excitement as Jim fiddled with the aerial, trying to point it directly at the satellite for the best link. It turned out that Mum, Vicky, Steve, Ryan, Bronny, Ben, Murray and Jim's sister Betty were all there. Apparently they could hear us loud and clear but we couldn't hear them too well. Their voices were often broken and garbled or just 'dropped out'. Jim and I were frustrated at not being able to have a conversation with our family, and I was on the brink of tears by the time we lost our fourth connection.

When we announced to the crew that the Sat M was up and running there was a constant trickle of visitors knocking on the door of the hut to use the phone. We warned them that the link could be dodgy but that didn't put them off. They all had better luck than we did and were able to make reasonably good connections. It was lovely to see the guys when they contacted their wives and kids – they were all beaming. It was a bit awkward for them talking from such a crowded 'public phone booth', but there just wasn't any place you could go in Gadget Hut for privacy. It was obvious that everyone was missing home after almost a month's absence, although it felt more as if a lifetime had passed since we left civilisation. Knowing that everyone at home was getting on with their normal life in the sweltering Aussie summer, while we were living among the ice and blizzards, made us all feel worlds away.

On Monday 25 January I realised that it was the first day of the new school year. I rang my school at Balnarring at mid-morning to say hello and to let them know that I had arrived safely, and to wish them all a happy start to the year. The line was pretty good this time and everyone I spoke to was genuinely excited to receive their first call from Antarctica. Graeme Sweatman, our principal, said that they had seen our departure from Hobart on the television news, and that my dark glasses hadn't hidden the tears. He said that he'd pass on my hellos to the kids at assembly the following day and assured me that there'd be plenty of e-mail messages flying across the airwaves as soon as we got our system working.

Once the hut was fully commissioned and Jim was convinced that everything was operating well, we took time out to have some fun with the crew. All the action was around Mawson's Hut. A few of the guys were making like archaeologists, digging an enormous deep hole into a snowdrift about 30 metres from the hut. Rob Easther of the Antarctic Division had told us about a tent that had been abandoned last summer during the restoration work. The blizzards had become so bad that a quick evacuation from the Cape was required and they'd had to leave a lot of equipment behind. Rob had said that inside the tent were boxes of tools used to work on the hut and he'd asked that if we found them they be returned to Tasmania on *Spirit*. John made it his personal mission to retrieve every item left in the ice. I've never seen a man enjoy hard work as much as he did.

All that could be seen of the Weatherhaven tent was a few fragments of blue fabric protruding from the ice. The excavations revealed the tent poles still in position but the nylon shell had been shredded by the wind and torn from the frame. The interior of the tent was totally filled with densely compacted ice. After hours of chipping with a mattock and ice axe an incredible collection of gear was discovered, including a full-size wheelbarrow. Great cries of delight from John accompanied each find and his excitement was contagious as each article was extracted from its icy grave.

Steve and Harry were also excavating, but they were trying to find Mawson's front door. The entire western side of the old hut had a two metre ice buildup which meant they couldn't access the entrance. Steve, Jim and I had been granted a permit to enter the hut in order to install a series of sensors and a data logger for the Australian Museum, which had requested our assistance during our time on the Cape. It appeared that just finding the way inside was going to be the first challenge.

The good weather was beginning to end. The temperatures had started to drop noticeably and the winds had begun blowing longer and harder. Dave made the decision that it was time to get out before things became really nasty and announced that everything had to be made ready to sail on the next calm day.

On the night of 26 January (Australia Day) Jim and I were invited on board for a farewell dinner. The four day blizzard we had been experiencing had blown itself out for a while and the Cape was eerily quiet. It was wonderful tramping down to the pick-up point on Boat Harbour for our night out. The surface of the snow crunched beneath our boots and the air was crispy cold. The evening sky was deep blue with a few fluffy white clouds scudding across it. It felt so-o-o good to be out!

Guy stood on the rocks waiting for us at 10pm and carefully stowed the freshly baked loaf of bread I'd brought along as a gift. We could smell the roast lamb as we approached *Spirit*. Mmmmm! Below decks it was warm, crowded and friendly. It was so nice being there with everyone as we talked, ate, drank and laughed together. They were such a great bunch of blokes. Jim and I had really enjoyed their company on the trip south and during the days we had spent together on the continent. I had mixed feelings about their imminent departure. I knew that I would miss them, but I was really eager to begin my year of isolation.

We left *Spirit* for the last time at one in the morning. Steve presented us with a parting gift of the last five cans of Coke on board. We received them happily and said we would mark each of them with the date of a special occasion and put them away until then. Dave gave us a large snaplock bag full of chocolate bars. He'd been aghast when he heard that we only had twelve blocks of chocolate for the whole year!

The light was flat and 'twilightish' as we motored away from the yacht. The water surface was greasy looking, already at the first stage of freezing over. When the motor was cut we drifted through heavier pancake ice for the last few metres to the rocks. Stomping back over the ice towards Gadget Hut, our arms laden with goodies and our tummies full of food and whisky (thanks to Guy) was a heavenly feeling. The open sky was pink and grey and the clouds a gorgeous shade of mauve. Our frozen breath hung around us as we stopped to wave to Guy. We glanced across at one another and just smiled. This was one of those times when there was no need to say anything at all.

We awoke to another marvellous day. The breeze was a gentle 20 km/h and the sky clear and blue without a cloud to be seen. 'Perfect sailing weather, I think,' Jim declared as he looked out of our frosty window. Dave radioed to tell us that *Spirit* was leaving early that evening if the conditions held. We raced down to help with any last minute tasks before they got underway. I took our oversized Aussie flag with me and we all posed with it in front of 'Doug's Place' – Mawson's Hut – for the final group photo. I gave Dave a bagful of films that he'd promised to take back to Australia for us. He said he'd send them on to Murray, along with some personal letters I'd written for friends. It was quick hugs all round and fond words of encouragement before the last crew members climbed into the yacht and dropped the mooring lines. *Spirit* motored quietly into Commonwealth Bay.

The air was Antarctic warm with barely a breeze, and the sea was still, reflecting the deep colour of the sky. I wondered how the crew felt about leaving such a magnificent place behind. A few had said to me earlier that they could almost understand how I could want to spend a year here. I was stunned, I thought that all of them would kill to change places with me! I knew that Dave was keen to be going, though: his worst nightmare was being caught in a week-long blizzard, unable to leave *Spirit*, and *Spirit* unable to leave Boat Harbour.

The view as they left must have been impressive, particularly as they retraced the line of stunning ice cliffs around Commonwealth Bay. We saw them in full sail as they neared the horizon about two hours after motoring out. *Spirit* looked magnificent in all her glory as she slowly headed north. I felt strangely empty as I whispered: 'Have a safe journey home.'

Now that the yacht had gone I was committed, unable to change my mind and seek the refuge of the 'real world' again. I had to face whatever came my way. Could Jim and I outlast this kind of ordeal and not come to hate each other? We already thought that we knew each other intimately, but this sort of experience could really find us out. I wondered what would happen if we reached a time in the year when we had nothing else to reveal to each other, when we were able to anticipate each other's thoughts and actions and there were no more little surprises. The risks were great, but none that I could foresee were too great. Antarctica was no reckless whim. It was something I had dreamed about, imagined and thought over for many years.

Now that it felt as though we had the whole continent to ourselves my heart rate quickened. This was it! I wondered what might occur in our lives between now and when we saw the yacht return. Whatever happened we were on our own now and would have to cope unassisted.

When the men on *Spirit* became mere yellow dots on deck Jim ran towards me, grinning wildly. He threw his arms around me and we fell together onto the slushy snow. I thought, we're going to have a great year!

6.

Doug's Place

After huddling together on the rocks at the furthest tip of the Cape watching *Spirit of Sydney* disappear over the horizon, we scurried back to the warmth of Gadget Hut to indulge ourselves Antarctic-style by declaring it bath night. With no basic plumbing facilities our birdbath-in-a-bucket didn't really come up to the standards we always took for granted at home. But when it's all you've got you learn to make the most of it.

Jim offered to heat the water on the stove-top because, I hate to admit, I was scared of the stove. I had left behind my electric stove and double wall ovens and traded them for a two-burner kerosene monster! To light the damn thing you had to prime it with methylated spirits before pumping the fuel cylinder with a bicycle pump to ensure that there was enough pressure to fill the tubes with fuel. The trouble was that I just couldn't get the hang of how much priming the jets needed and consequently great yellow flames used to flare halfway up the wall, making the hut reek of kerosene and smoke before I could turn it off and throw the door open. I was beginning to believe that my inadequacies at the stove were going to be the biggest hazard to our safety in Antarctica – I'd either burn the place down or we'd starve to death. Finally I learned how to light it.

I collected the bath bucket, gel and shampoo and hung the towel over the heater to warm up. As each kettle boiled we filled the three thermos flasks we referred to as our hot water system. The flame was hot, but the water was so cold in the kettle that it took an hour to get enough warm water to begin bathing.

For some time I had been eyeing Jim's unruly hair and now offered to trim it a bit while we were waiting. He agreed to this but put a ban on touching his beard. He said he was going for the Ned Kelly look and wasn't going to touch it until we arrived back home in the new millennium. I suspected that when it began freezing up in his balaclava he'd change his mind, but I didn't say anything. I hunted out my brand new, ultrasharp hairdressing scissors that I'd brought especially to help us keep some semblance of good grooming while down south. I didn't want to send digital images back to the 'real world' with us looking as if we'd spent all of our life in the wild.

As I trimmed away the fluffy bits growing around Jim's sideburns and ears he sat rigidly still. He was apparently terrified that I was going to slip and cut his ears off or stab him with the points. He offered to reciprocate, but I declined the gesture and decided on the spot that I would grow my hair and tie it up in a ponytail. The short back and sides Jim offered didn't appeal to me.

It's amazing how much brighter life is when you have a clean, sweet-smelling body and freshly shampooed hair. The six litres of warm water we each used for our ablutions had been well used – we not only managed a shampoo and birdbath but our undies had been washed too and hung over the heater to dry. Feeling unusually good, we poured ourselves a nip of Bundy, and with no shortage of ice we sat back to soak up the ambience. I felt so happy and content that I had to pinch myself to be sure that we'd actually begun to live our dream and that this was reality.

Since crossing the Antarctic Circle a few weeks before (Harry won that bet too!) our reluctance to go to bed had increased as the hours of night-time darkness decreased. It got to the point where we were still wandering around or working at three or four o'clock most mornings. Time had become irrelevant, but in an effort to re-establish more normal waking and sleeping patterns, and to keep in sync with Melbourne time, we discussed the need to discipline ourselves to going to bed before midnight and getting up around seven.

Antarctica doesn't have any time zones, so for convenience we chose to stay with Australian Eastern Standard Time. We didn't have an alarm clock with us so we were relying on our rather confused internal clocks to wake us. The sun was as bright as day when we flung ourselves up on to the bunk and snuggled in among the layers of goosedown. Jim thought that he'd take advantage of the light and do a spot of reading in bed before going to sleep. He must have lasted a full 30 seconds before he threw his book on the table below and wrapped the bed covers around his frozen arms.

Waiting for sleep to come, I lay watching the penguins through the tiny window over the stove. I had a direct view of a busy rookery located on the rocks between Commonwealth Bay and us. Activity in Adelie rookeries continues 24 hours a day during this time of year when the new generation of penguins are growing with astonishing rapidity. At this stage in their cycle the chicks are already the size of their parents but still covered by thick, charcoal-coloured down coats. Until they shed the down for their new slick adult plumage they must not get wet and are totally reliant on their parents for food. Both parents spend long hours out at sea to keep them fed so the big chicks are left in communal creches, watched by surrogate aunties and uncles. The parent birds scour the sea, stuffing themselves with krill, only to disgorge it down their hungry youngsters' throats back at the nest before waddling to the shore and moving out to sea again.

Watching sleepily, I saw a real life drama unfold and sat almost upright in the chilly hut to get a better view. A large brown predatory skua appeared menacingly at the edge of the rookery. He was about the size and bulk of a hawk and with his wings spread wide looked absolutely huge and threatening. He ran at a group of penguins, lunged forward and grabbed a large fluffy chick with his sharp beak. To my horror the chick squawked and flapped its flippers futilely as the skua dragged it away from the others. The rest of the penguins huddled together tightly and watched the chick try to escape time and time again. Instinct must have told them that they were powerless to help the doomed chick and no one moved a centimetre. It took several minutes for the death struggles to cease; then the predator began to devour the chick. By now the band of frightened Adelies had moved over a little rise together and turned their backs on the brutal scene.

Fascinated and appalled, I watched as the giant bird began pulling chunks out of the soft fat baby, its little tufts of grey down flying away with the breeze to land on the pure white snow nearby.

Four more skuas descended from the skies hoping to join the feast but were repelled aggressively. The awful thing is that this scene is repeated numerous times every day over the short summer, and has done so for thousands of years. I reminded myself that in the wild this was all part of natural selection, ensuring that only the fittest survive to pass on their genes to the following generations. Life for the penguins was no picnic and they needed incredible strength and will to survive in the harshest environment on Earth. I rolled closer to Jim's warm body and tried to sleep.

It was my turn to get up first in the morning. I had no sense of what time it was and felt annoyed to discover that we'd overslept our planned 7am rising time and that it was nearer to 10am. So much for our great plans! It might take a while to get the new routine right. I had had a fairly uncomfortable night and my sleep was broken. It dawned on me about two hours after turning off the heater and getting into bed that shampooing my hair at night time was not a smart thing to do. My half frozen head woke me up several times with severe 'ice cream headache' symptoms. In the end I had jammed a hat over my icy locks, seeking warmth, and lapsed into a deep sleep.

Although I wore a set of light thermals, the shock of the temperature change had me shivering in seconds as I slid down from the bed onto the table before lowering myself to the floor. All of last night's discarded clothes were draped over my bench seat so I hurriedly put them on again in order to dash out to the annex. On my way past the automatic weather station gauge I pressed the 'indoor temperature' button to discover that it was minus 3°C.

Apart from housing an extraordinary assortment of hardware, crates of cheese and margarine, bottles of fuel, a satellite aerial and a diesel generator, the annex was also home to our toilet bucket. It was the coldest room in the hut and usually the same temperature as outside. The freezer thermometer on the wall near the door showed minus 9°C, and the icicles crusted on the rim of the bucket confirmed that I shouldn't stay long! Back in the hut for a quick wash with last night's leftover thermos water, a bit of cream slapped on the face, a new hat on my head, and I was ready to begin my day.

I lit the kero heater and put the kettle on for the best cup of coffee of the day. One fuel leak and three flare-ups later I had a lovely blue flame burning on the stove. I opened two of the hut's air vents to keep the air sweet and safe to breathe (if not a little cold) then fossicked around for breakfast food before calling Jim.

The fresh yoghurt I had made the day before was frozen solid in the container on the bench, so breakfast consisted of a huge bowl of steaming porridge cooked with loads of dried fruit, cinnamon and milk powder. Our dietitian had emphasised the need to keep our calcium intake up. I was struggling to adjust to drinking powdered milk, so I added it to our cooking at every available chance.

While eating, Jim downloaded the weather station statistics for the past 24 hours. That night we'd had wind gusts of over 80 km/h but they were beginning to slacken off as we approached midday. The barometer was reading 988 millibars and rising. We predicted that we were in for a spell of good weather. With that in mind we agreed to get our chores out of the way as quickly as possible and spend the rest of the afternoon exploring.

Most of our gear was inside the hut with us. After unpacking and storing all we could on the packing case shelves and in all the nooks and crannies, we took a visual stocktake. What we saw satisfied us.

The place was even more cramped than before, chockfull of books, food, cooking equipment, spare parts, batteries, stationery, games, repair kits and cameras. Leads, wires, transformers and rechargers were draped around the room, which meant that we had to be careful about untangling ourselves in rising from the table. Most importantly, though, we had the means of a safe and secure existence. Everything was handy in our world that we could cross in two or three paces. It wasn't a luxurious world but we were ecstatically happy.

The upside of this was that not much housework was required in a room resembling the inside of a garden shed. The old routine of tidying, vacuuming, dusting and mopping was replaced with sweeping the floor and a quick wipe of the table. As if to counterbalance the ease and speed of these basic housework tasks we were continually faced with the grind of the dreaded 'bucket run'. At the start of the year that only meant emptying the slops bucket (with its grey water from the sink) and our toilet bucket into the waters of Commonwealth Bay. Within a few short weeks, daily filling of the snow bucket ready for melting into water would also be included in our routine.

All our hard rubbish had to be sorted into three categories: cans and jars, paper and cardboard, and plastics. Prior to leaving Australia we'd tried to eliminate as much packaging as possible by removing unnecessary cellophane wrappers and cardboard boxes. We were staggered by the amount we were able to discard without compromising the quality of the contents. We regularly compacted and double-wrapped our rubbish in heavy duty plastic before sledding it over to Granholm Hut for storage. The hard rubbish would be returning to Australia with us for disposal or recycling. Storing it in the old ANARE hut beside Boat Harbour meant that it would be quicker and easier to ferry it across to *Spirit* next January. This early in the year we didn't appear to have much to store, and we wondered how many bags we would end up with when the yacht returned. I'd never thought before about what a year's worth of rubbish would look like.

Carting a 25 litre bucket brimming with waste across the ice to the edge of Commonwealth Bay sounds like no great hardship. Add to that, however, the need to fully gear up with protective clothing before opening the door of the hut, and the icy Antarctic wind gusts that battered us the moment we stepped outside, and the chore became more taxing and time consuming. It was always very satisfying, though, to tip the waste into the sea and head back with empty buckets knowing that we were set for another day or two.

The water level in our barrel was below the tap line after the night's splurge with the bath bucket, so we loaded the four empty water containers onto a sled and trudged up the slope behind our hut to resupply from the frozen lakes. Cape Denison has six such lakes that remain permanently frozen all year round. Long Lake and Round Lake were the closest to our hut and we learned later that Mawson's team also collected water there all those years ago.

The lake surface has a permanent cover of ice, which becomes thicker as the air temperature drops. Because the floating ice is always freezing underneath and evaporating on top, the ice crystals are aligned vertically. The result of this phenomenon is sunlight being transmitted down into unbelievably clear water below. The surface of the lakes reminded me of decorative glass bricks with millions of tiny air bubbles frozen into place. Walking across them and peering down into their depths was a wonderfully unique experience that I never ceased to marvel at.

Our ice axes were able to chip through the layer of clear blue ice relatively easily, and as the water percolated to the surface we scooped it up with a saucepan and siphoned it into the barrels. A small band of Adelies, passing through on their way down to the harbour for a swim, stopped to watch the goings on. The wind was howling across the frozen surface as we squatted beside the hole, nipping our fingers and blowing icy water all over the barrels and us. Ice layers began to build up on each barrel and our clothing. It took us two and a half hours to collect the 80 litres we needed for the hut. It was worth it, though, because it would have taken us a lot more time and precious fuel to melt enough snow to make such a quantity of fresh water. This felt like a gift and we intended to take advantage of what we could extract from the lakes for as long as possible.

Both Jim and I were keen to spend time exploring around Mawson's Hut while the rocks and relics around the outside were still exposed. Although it was only the end of January I had seen many photos of the historical site and I knew that for most of the year ice and snow blew in from the south and all but buried everything. We felt we had a lot of serious fossicking to do before that happened so I stuffed my pockets with dried fruit bars, Jim grabbed the cameras, and we headed across the valley.

The sun was still high in the sky and there was barely a puff of wind as we made our way across the ice sheet towards the hut. On arriving I realised that we had forgotten to take our ice axes or a shovel, so we couldn't get in the front door. We weren't too disappointed as we had our cameras and shot some of the interesting 'junk' in the rocks around the hut. All the artefacts have been meticulously documented by a Sydney archaeologist working for the AAP Mawson's Hut Foundation, so we were very careful not to disturb or dislodge anything.

The ice around Doug's Place had thawed enough to reveal that back in 1912 they must have cared little for their immediate environment because they dumped and abandoned a plethora of disused items. We found poking through the snow, or sheltered among the boulders, discarded clothing, bits of timber, an old leather boot, a section of sled, pieces of coal, hundreds of metres of wire, animal bones, crates of rusty food cans, and piles of penguin and seal carcasses. Jim was very excited at finding the old weathered Oregon mast and tangled wires which had enabled the first radio transmissions to be made from Antarctica. Fascinated by the remnants of a bygone era, Jim and I spent hours looking around trying to identify each piece and reconstruct its story.

My thoughts wandered to how important the site is in Australia's Antarctic history. Sir Douglas and his party of 18 men built the main hut and three smaller huts in 1912. The expedition stayed on Cape Denison until December 1913, having explored by sledge and ship more than 1100 km of coastline and penetrated 400 km inland. This was the very spot where Mawson began what is arguably the most remarkable journey by any known explorer, and I was humbled to be there.

It seemed tragic that after 86 years there was still no firm decision on the long-term future of the hut. Back in the mid-1980s a private expedition named Project Blizzard did some maintenance work on Mawson's Hut and produced comprehensive documentation on its condition. Then, until recently, no real measures were taken to restore and maintain the hut.

The huts built by Borchrevnik, Scott and Shackleton in other parts of the continent have been preserved and restored to close to their original condition. I felt a deep sense of sadness that this wonderful piece of our Antarctic heritage was being lost despite Cape Denison's inclusion in the Antarctic Treaty List of Historic Monuments. The scene before us clearly illustrated that the infamous Cape Denison katabatic winds were eroding the Baltic pine timbers and scattering anything loose far and wide across the Cape and out into Commonwealth Bay.

The current conservation program involves cooperative efforts by AAP Mawson's Hut Foundation, the Australian Heritage Commission and the Australian Antarctic Division. Happily they are all committed to ensuring that the site is preserved, and our installing scientific equipment on top of Gadget Hut and the datalogger in Mawson's Hut played an important part in their program. From the data we collected and e-mailed back to the scientists at the National Museum of Australia and the Australian Museum they would determine the effect of temperature, humidity, solar rays and ingress of drift on the deterioration of the hut. This information will allow them to make more accurate decisions on what action to take next.

I now noticed for the first time that afternoon that Commonwealth Bay was clotted with chunks of ice. The bergy bits scattered around were quite large and crashed into one another as they rode the waves. There were long lines of slushy ice extending kilometres across the bay. As salt water has a lower freezing point than fresh water it must have been excruciatingly cold out there. It didn't seem to worry the Adelies, though – they were springing in and out at the water's edge like kids on a beach. Some were having a little rest on the chunks floating out in the bay, trying to keep their balance as they rode the heavy swell. The massive Wedell seals with their thick layers of blubber were lolling around on icy islands too, with hardly a shiver among them. Again I was reminded of how magnificently these animals have adapted to this frozen environment.

My eyes felt intensely itchy so I removed my goggles and began rubbing my eyes with my mitts. I realised that it may have had something to do with leaving the goggles in my pocket for about an hour and a half while I photographed around the hut. Perhaps this was the first stage of snowblindness. I had heard snowblindness described as 'sunburn of the retina'. The reflected glare off the ice will give a severe dose of sunburn to the skin, so the effects on the eyes would be the same. I vowed to be more careful.

Hunger distracted us from our treasure hunt. We had polished off the dried fruit ages ago, so we collected our cameras and strolled home to eat. We had no idea what the time was as neither of us bothered to wear a watch any more. The sun was high over the McKeller Islands and it felt like late afternoon, but in reality it was almost 8pm when we entered the hut. We planned to have a meal and then return with ice axes and shovels to dig our way into Mawson's Hut. Jim also wanted to connect some CSIRO sensors to the datalogger and check that the rest of the equipment that Steve and Harry had installed was still working properly.

Jim flicked on the HF radio to see if we could pick up *Spirit*'s 8pm sked with Casey Station. Hard bursts of static and electronic squeals filled the hut but it was great to hear Dave's voice once again while he spoke to Bob Orchard, the radio operator at Casey. He said that the crew was already noticing the warmer temperatures on deck as they sailed away from the continent. Today they basked in a 'tropical' 4°C – it was minus 4°C here. A few guys on board had had a close call with carbon monoxide poisoning after running the stove with the cabin door closed. Fortunately the group on watch noticed and opened the door and all of the hatches. They were on their way to the South Magnetic Pole and hoped to arrive in Hobart in about a week.

We tried to communicate with *Spirit* too but they couldn't pick up our signal and we had to give up when Dave signed off. We never had much luck all year in transmitting messages on the HF radio. A weekly sked had been organised with the radio operator at Casey, just so we could chat regularly to others and share news. I was terribly disappointed that we were never successful in our transmissions. We only managed to hear electronic crackling noises and had to abandon the idea after many unsuccessful attempts. Often throughout the year I thought how terrific that contact would have been with our closest Australian neighbours just 1500 kilometres up the coast.

It was four days before Jim and I could return to Mawson's Hut again. A blizzard suddenly started up and didn't allow us to get outside for anything other than the essentials of emptying our waste buckets and collecting another fuel drum for the hut. The snow was falling horizontally from the south rather than out of the sky, destined never to touch the ground as the wind gusts accelerated to 110 km/h.

Armed with all the digging equipment we would need, plus a couple of Dolphin torches, we arrived at the door of Doug's Place determined to get in and have a good look around. I noticed that the gaping hole left in the snow nearby after John's recent excavations had completely disappeared. There was a new smooth snow slope in its place and no sign of there having been any human presence. A small group of curious penguins returning from a fishing trip stopped and watched us shovel snow away and chip at the ice. I was surprised at how compacted the ice buildup was around the door when it had been cleared only a week ago. I unconsciously held my breath when Jim pushed the bolt aside and slowly opened the creaky old wooden door.

A large quantity of fine drift had found its way through the gaps between the door and its frame, so we had to carefully remove it before entering. To be able to get to the main hut we had to wend our way through an ice tunnel created by last year's working party. They had cut blocks of ice with a chain saw and removed them by hand to allow access to the inner sanctum of the hut.

We crawled over the metal box that contained the datalogger. It was set up just inside the front door. Taking care not to become tangled up in the multitude of sensor wires, we clicked on our torches and silently entered the tunnel. It was dark and cold as we twisted our way through the workshop towards the main hut. I stopped at one stage and turned back to face the light at the entrance. 'Wow, look at the crystals,' I gasped to Jim. 'The ceiling looks like one big chandelier.' The sunlight touching the millions of delicate, sparkling ice crystals growing on the walls and ceiling mesmerised me. It was the most beautiful room I had ever been in and it made me think that that's what Ali Baba's cave must have looked like. I turned back towards the darkness and followed Jim's disappearing light.

Suddenly the claustrophobic tunnel opened out into a large frozen cavern that I recognised as the Mawson team's living quarters. What a moment! We stood together and played our torch beams around the room before us. The light danced across the remaining ice and to our delight picked out the bunks, shelves and other treasures left behind so long ago. With the greatest of care not to strangle ourselves on the myriad wires draped around the place, and not to disturb anything else, we slowly shuffled around.

With our torchlight we picked out the bunks that lined the walls. Some were still entombed in ice but others revealed the initials of the original occupants, burnt into the wood with a hot poker. I couldn't find Ninnis and Mertz's bunks with their missing slats, but seeing the letters FJH brought sharp memories of Frank Hurley and his now famous collection of photographs. Jim and I must have seen every one of Hurley's brilliant Antarctic images that were ever published. We have a great admiration for the way he captured the essence of the 'heroic age'. Jim's remark, 'Look, there's Hurley's darkroom', made my heart nearly skip a beat. We opened the door and peeped inside to see a mess of abandoned chemicals and papers strewn around the shelves and floor.

Flashing our lights before us we made our way around the fingers of ice suspended from the loft and inspected the rows of shelves. We saw early 20th century paperbacks, an ancient gramophone record and old tins and jars, some with labels still intact and advertising Heinz relish and Keens mustard. On the floor were scattered some perfectly preserved spuds and several biology specimen jars with contents unrecognisable. And to my amazement a stuffed skua was hidden under one of the bunks. We could even see some items of woollen clothing protruding from the huge sections of ice still jammed between the roof and the floor.

At the southern end of the hut Jim located Mawson's private cubicle and we were thrilled to find that most of the ice had been removed from within and we could clearly identify his bunk with its ticking pillow. Mawson was a tall man and had made sure that his bunk was built to accommodate his lanky frame. Some of the others I had seen in the hut must have been used by midgets, because I wouldn't have been able to lie fully stretched on them. Doug's chair stood near his bed and various shelves that had held his books and scientific equipment covered the cubicle walls.

Feeling quite drained of emotion I was brought back to the present by the sight of the ever practical Jim beginning to systematically check each of the sensors throughout the hut. He was making sure that none had moved or fallen out of place. Making our way back through the tunnel we replaced the two snow baffle doors behind us to prevent any more drift entering the hut.

Crawling out of the front door into the dazzling sunlight felt like stepping out of a time warp. We lingered for a few minutes, wanting to hold on to the moment before closing the door and sealing it with shovelfuls of loose snow. We talked for ages that night, feeling a special closeness after having experienced something truly extraordinary together.

7.

Keeping Count

*I*n mid-February, just three short weeks after being left alone on Cape Denison, we were hit with a sudden onslaught of severe weather, which proved to be a prolonged spell. Although officially summer hadn't quite finished, I had a feeling that on our little stretch of Antarctic coastline, winter was definitely on the way. Already, for five days of each week, we'd endured wind gusts measuring over 100 km/h, and the average daily wind speed for the month was 75 km/h.

Airborne drift blown across the Cape frequently blotted out the sunlight and obscured our vision to only a few metres. Although we tried to avoid going outside in such conditions we were sometimes caught out when a sudden change roared in from the south. To find our way back to Gadget Hut we couldn't rely on following our tracks in the snow as they would often fill in with drift and disappear within seconds. Most of the time we could make out the dark shadows of the rocks and we used those as a guide for direction. The temperature began falling sharply, each week seeming colder than the one before. Our chilliest February day registered at minus 19°C.

I loved the blast of Antarctic weather and monitored it carefully on the weather station, always eager to discover the coldest temperatures and the strongest wind gusts. I figured that if it had to be cold, it might as well be a record. We knew that this was only a hint of what was to come and I was readily anticipating what was on offer. I had already experienced extremes of weather in the mountains of Nepal and New Zealand but that was only for weeks at a time. What would it be like for months on end? It looked as if I was about to find out sooner than I'd expected!

While Jim and I could sit out the blizzards in the safety and relative comfort of our hut, the poor Adelie penguins were left to struggle in the freezing cold. During February and March they were probably at their most vulnerable, as that's the period when they moult. The chicks replace their thick downy coats with smooth adult plumage, and the rest of the penguins replace their old feathers with new ones. During this time they cannot go out to sea to feed and have to live off their body fat until the moult is completed. The length of time required for this apparent metamorphosis to take place varies with each bird, but when the blizzards are howling around them, literally blowing the fluff off their backs, it must seem like an eternity. Once their slick new coat emerges they don't hang around for long. All penguins leave Cape Denison immediately their breeding and moulting cycle is complete, spending the next seven or eight months out at sea to escape the shocking weather on the continent.

One evening when Jim and I were making our way to Jubilee Base to set up the telescope lent to us by York Optical, we stumbled across a couple of largely deserted colonies with just a few small groups of Adelies, all at various stages of moult. It was obvious that they were doing it tough, crouched behind rocks for protection or standing hunched with their backs to the wind. The more we walked among them the worse it appeared. We saw penguins whose beaks had iced shut, so that they could no longer eat, drink or preen, and some had ice helmets that completely covered their heads. Flippers had been frozen to bodies, many bleeding where they had been pecked in a desperate effort to free them. Most of the birds had ice crusts on their backs so thick that they formed frozen armour plates.

As the unfortunate penguins shuffled around, the ice on their backs cracked into segments and looked like a turtle's shell covering them from head to tail. One little fellow was so heavily laden that he couldn't support his own weight, his legs buckling as he got up to waddle away. I was disturbed to note that he wasn't doing anything to try to improve his sad condition. I guessed that he had given up. He just sat with his back to the wind and every gust of drift that hit him added to the already burdensome accumulation of ice on his body. His prospects for survival didn't look good.

We felt sure that many of the penguins wouldn't live through the sudden wintry conditions. The weather was likely to get worse rather than better, and we didn't like the birds' chances. Jim and I talked about helping one unfortunate penguin that had great, heavy clumps of ice hanging like pendulums from his neck feathers. Each time he tried to waddle the hanging lumps shifted, threw him off balance and caused him to fall over. We thought that we could easily remove the ice clumps and improve his chances of getting to the open sea and surviving another season, but we knew it was wrong to interfere. I ached with sadness as we reluctantly tore ourselves away from the struggling birds and walked on. I felt angry at how cruel nature can be.

The weeks passed quickly and the blizzards regularly worked their way into a frenzy, followed by brief spells of gorgeous calm. During that time we learned how sturdy and sound our little hut was. Twelve steel guy-wires were attached to metal plates around the roofline and secured to the rocks with chains. After a big blow we would always check that each wire was still taut and make any adjustments needed to keep the hut as stable as possible. Inside were two reinforcing bars added after construction to brace the roof and the southern wall, which had an unnerving tendency to flex inwards as the wind gusts pounded.

Because the hut was constructed of prefabricated panels fitted together with aluminium H-beams, it was always a nagging worry that if struck too hard a panel might give way and the entire hut implode. In my imagination I could see it disintegrate and blow away like a house of cards. I took great comfort from knowing that Gadget Hut was a veteran of four Antarctic winters and hoped that it would manage to ride through this one too.

Part of our Dis-Plan was for both Jim and me to have an emergency pack filled with all the basic requirements for our immediate survival in case such a disaster occurred. These packs had to be readily accessible in an emergency and were stored behind our bench seats where we could grab them in the event of an evacuation. We also had items of clothing, food and other gear stored at Jubilee Base in case a fire destroyed our hut and everything inside.

The daily bucket run was more than a chore at that time – it was becoming downright dangerous. With winds regularly gusting between 70 and 110 km/h I had to keep alert to stay on my feet. The sudden force would first strike us the moment we left the lee of the hut, and from then on it was a battle to get down to the water's edge and back safely. Often when a particularly strong gust roared down the valley between our dumping site and the hut, I had to squat down low to present the smallest resistance possible rather than be knocked down by the blast.

I had learned not to *sit* when a gust came through, because on occasions I'd been blown along the ice on my bottom, desperately hanging on to the handle of my bucket and trying not to allow the contents to slop over the rim. I usually got an attack of the giggles when caught unawares like that. Jim's worried body language as he watched helplessly would make me laugh even more. He took to walking beside me, placing his own body in such a way that he took the full brunt of the wind. He often had to grab the tail of my jacket or a flailing arm just to keep me from blowing away. No wonder we got back exhausted after each trip. I was usually exhilarated but Jim's concern grew. 'It's time we put the blizz lines in,' he declared.

On the next calm day we collected our two metre aluminium poles from beneath the hut, headed down to the dumping site, and thrust a pole securely into the compacted snow every ten paces leading back to the hut. The idea was that if caught in a serious whiteout we could find our way along the pole line to safety. We had no idea at that stage that some of the poles would be all but buried under snowdrifts later in the year, leaving only inconspicuous and useless tips poking through the surface.

At the actual dumping site we established a row of stronger steel poles and secured a bright orange 6 mm line along them.

We planned to tether ourselves to the line to avoid being blown over the edge and into the water. We had each stitched a body harness between the lining and the outer shell of our jackets and clipped on a carabiner (a metal locking device) to attach to the tether. It was obvious that the ice ledges were building up rapidly and were already metres above the waves of Commonwealth Bay. If one of us ended up in the water it would be impossible to get out before hypothermia overpowered us.

Drift had been getting into every fold and crease of our Gore-Tex outer clothing. Any little gap, no matter how minute, allowed the ice and wind in and chilled us – the sensation progressing from cold to searing pain. It was time to make some modifications that would seal us into our protective clothing better. We also made an extra effort when gearing up to ensure that every layer we wore was tucked in, zipped up and Velcroed securely. No more shortcuts!

Our heavier and more wind-resistant clothes were unpacked at around that time and added to our 'summer wardrobe'. Jim brought out his windstopper facemask and sheepskin 'Biggles' hat as well. I also hunted out my facemask, but I didn't think that Antarctica was ready for my sheepskin hat yet. When Jim and I bought the hats months before at the Victoria Market we thought they would be fantastically warm but made a secret pact never to film each other wearing them. That didn't stop us laughing hysterically every time we put them on.

Living in the windiest place on Earth meant that when a calm spell arrived it had quite an unsettling effect on us. We found the unusual stillness eerie; the sudden periods of quiet startled us. We would strain to hear something, anything, in the unfamiliar silence. Another change that frequently came with the calm was the way lovely dry flakes of snow fluttered down from the sky rather than hurtling horizontally with the katabatic wind. Huge dumps could arrive within hours, covering everything on the Cape, turning the landscape totally white – rocks, penguins and the rapidly freezing sea. Early in March we were awakened from a deep sleep, alarmed by a sudden quiet. The only sound was the gentle patter of snow on the hut's roof. As we scrambled into our jackets and poked our heads out the door we were delighted to find the Cape being transformed before our eyes. The chill air sent us back to bed but when we arose in the morning we were amazed to find a two metre blanket of snow around the hut.

We had great fun trying to walk around in the deep drifts, disappearing up to our waist in places and floundering around like beached seals. We were disappointed to discover that snowballs wouldn't hold together, so we had to throw handfuls of the frozen stuff at each other. I later read that in extremely cold, dry environments like Antarctica the snowflakes resemble grains of sand in shape and don't have the spiky profile that allows them to be squashed into snowballs. What a shame!

It dawned on me slowly as I was playing on the slope behind the hut that there wasn't a trace of the food boxes we had stashed along the western wall. I thought that, if left, the snow might compact down and make retrieval of the boxes difficult in the future, so using a plastic dustpan to dig and scrape with I began clearing them. I checked that none were missing, then untied the next fortnight's boxes and took them inside.

Every carton was boldly numbered so they could be located easily and opened sequentially to ensure that our special birthday and anniversary boxes turned up at the right time. I saw that numbers 42 and 45 were looking a bit soggy and were stoved in at the corners. Those two had sat in water most of the way down from Hobart and I'd noticed they were suffering a bit when we unloaded *Spirit*. So now I broke with tradition and brought them inside instead of numbers 7 and 8. Slashing through the outside layers revealed a dry plastic inner bag securely protecting the contents. As I emptied the boxes and stacked the food on the table I was mortified to discover that in week 45 we would be eating exactly the same things as we had been eating during the first six weeks!

In planning the year's food it had been vital that we strike the right balance – that is, enough to satisfy us and keep us well fed and healthy, but not so much that our stores might sink the yacht. I'd thought that the most practical way to achieve that balance was to work out every meal we'd consume in Antarctica and pack accordingly. We planned for 365 breakfasts, 365 lunches and 365 dinners – a total of 1095 meals – plus 730 snacks. Wow! Our second year's food supply was already on the Cape courtesy of Don and Margie McIntyre.

By grouping the meals into one-week blocks I was able to get a better grip on what seemed like a mammoth task. Hence the weekly food box idea. Each carton was to hold everything we would eat during that week. That way I was confident there'd be enough food to last us the year, and we wouldn't be able to raid our supplies when we had an attack of the munchies and be left with all the grungy food at the end of the year.

Our maths was sorely tested as we worked out our daily intake of sugar, powdered milk, Vegemite, olive oil, tomato sauce and many other everyday food items. I was conscious that our calculations had to be right because once we arrived in Antarctica the closest convenience store would be an inconvenient 2500 km away. When calculating how many tea bags to take we began by deciding how many we would use each day, multiplied it by seven to get the weekly total, and then multiplied that by 52 to arrive at the year's consumption.

It all sounded great in theory but the reality was that we made some goof-ups. I based the quantity of tea and coffee on how much I normally bought at the supermarket each week, forgetting that Jim and I drank most of our tea and coffee each day at work. It didn't take long after arriving on the ice to realise that we were in for some rationing. We took to recycling the tea bags by hanging them over the heater after each use and using them a number of times before discarding them. The record for a single Earl Grey tea bag was eight cups of tea! Our coffee had to be restricted to one cup a day. We made that the first hot drink of the morning as an incentive for getting out of bed.

We'd been unsure about glass containers being able to survive in the cold so we tested various jars of food by placing them in the freezer at home to see if the glass and the contents could survive. Most did. To maximise variety we asked friends to tell us what food they couldn't live without and we included those in our stores too. Rhonda's passion for liquorice meant that we had a real treat during the year, but I have to admit that the jars of sauerkraut and pickled onions suggested by others weren't a big hit.

After stacking the contents of boxes 42 and 45 on the hut's shelves, I looked for the ingredients needed for dinner that night. The cans sitting in the packing cases had already begun to show the effects of the big freeze. The ends were swelling and I noticed that the contents of some of the jars were seeping out from under the lids. That made for some interesting smells in the hut! Cans or jars required for an evening meal already had to be thawed on top of the heater before the contents could be removed. If meat was on the menu, it had to be pegged on the rack above the heater to defrost.

I fancied spaghetti bolognaise so I first took an onion from the crate in the annex and allocated it a warm spot on the heater. It was frozen solid and felt like a cold, hard cricket ball in my hand. I didn't expect it to have much flavour, as the last few frozen onions were virtually tasteless and quite rubbery when cooked. I was adamant that I'd enjoy the 'fresh' food while I had it available, so it was probably just as well that this was the last onion – all we had then was a handful of old potatoes. I also put jars of crushed garlic and tomato paste, a bottle of olive oil and a can of tomatoes on top of the crowded heater where they could unfreeze. The cask of red wine was brought down from the top shelf and relocated closer to the heater. Red is usually best served at room temperature but as our hut was averaging 5°C during the day we opted for something warmer. I checked that I still had dried mushrooms and plenty of herbs, before gearing up, grabbing the snow shovel and venturing outside to dig up some meat.

Jim had finished digging the fuel barrels out of the deep new snow and suggested that while the food was thawing out we visit our seal neighbours around Boat Harbour. We liked to wander over there regularly to keep tabs on the wildlife in that area. The rocky ridges and icy valleys surrounding the harbour held the greatest variety of

Antarctic wildlife anywhere on the Cape. Populations of penguins and seals were the most prolific, but skuas, Antarctic petrels, snow petrels, tiny Wilson storm petrels and the very unattractive giant-petrels could be found there too. While the penguin population was diminishing as the season wore on, for some reason the seal numbers were on the increase. Last time we were down there we counted 70 Wedell seals lazing around the water's edge, totally oblivious to the punishing winds screaming around them.

No open water was visible on this occasion, as the calm conditions had allowed the millions of suspended ice particles floating beneath the surface to merge and consolidate and to form a solid ice layer across the entire harbour. Peering cautiously over the ice ledges I could see the frozen mass beneath me rising and falling gently with the swells.

Close by, a group of 15 Wedells were flaked out on the shore, totally unaware of our presence. These seals grow to around three metres in length and weigh as much as 400 kg. Fortunately they are known to be gentle giants with a wonderfully placid nature. This lot were catching some serious ZZZ's and only moving occasionally to stretch lazily or delicately scratch their tummies with a flipper. What a life! I almost envied them until I thought about the icy oceans that they swam around in and their diet of cold raw fish! No wonder seal burps smell like a newly opened can of sardines.

Quietly I crept closer to a young pup snoozing beside its mother. It looked so warm and pudgy with its thick layer of blubber forming deep creases around its soft velvety neck. It must have been dreaming because it was wriggling and jerking and making soft sucking noises in its sleep just like any other baby.

Jim clambered to a high point and began counting the seals. He was keeping records of the numbers in a log and was keen to get a figure. We often found that our first counts were inaccurate, as a large sleeping Wedell looks just like a rock and can be easily missed. It wasn't until we actually walked around the harbour, looking carefully at all the rocks, that our numbers became more realistic.

Jim called 'Check out the big fellow!' and pointed to a seal returning from a swim. It was trying to pull itself clumsily onto the floating ice in the harbour. It took a monumental effort to haul its massive body out of the water and launch itself on the ice. I watched delightedly while it wriggled around trying to get comfortable, ready for a snooze. Soon it was still and must have collapsed into a deep sleep because it was oblivious to the fact that it had begun to sink slowly. Its body heat was turning the newly formed ice into slush and within minutes it sank back into the water and disappeared. It must have decided to try again further around the point because we didn't see it again. Including the sinking seal we counted 62 Wedells and three crabeater seals on the shore.

To avoid the deepest snow, which was heavy going and very tiring to walk through, Jim and I returned to the hut by cutting across the rocks at the base of Penguin Knob. Most of the rookeries around there were completely abandoned, but some still held a few scruffy, miserable-looking penguins shedding their final feathers. As we walked across the rocks we were surprised at the number of penguin carcasses we stumbled over. There would have been hundreds in that area alone. Some were quite ancient but still in an amazing condition as the cold slowed down the deterioration process. Others had succumbed to the recent cold snap and looked as if they were simply resting on the ice. Many were obviously victims of skua attacks. These bodies were a macabre sight, not much more than skeletons, but always with their rubbery flippers and tough feet intact.

Jumping from rock to rock, making our way around the coast, we kept coming across fresh blood spatters on the clean white snow. There was never a sign of a struggle, which would have indicated that penguins had been killed there, so we were totally bamboozled as to where the blood had come from. I hurried back to Gadget Hut to consult my few Antarctic reference books. When Jim entered the hut, shaking the snow from his clothes, I announced grandly: 'It's giant-petrel vomit, not blood after all!'

Five very large, ugly giant-petrels had been staying with us on the Cape over the past month and we often saw them giving the skuas a hard time by attempting to steal their kill. Giant-petrels are carrion eaters and scavengers that have developed an unusual tactic for repelling other birds and claiming their prey – they vomit bright red oil mixed with the contents of their stomachs. I'll bet it works too!

Glancing at the ship's clock hanging on the wall above the door I was surprised to find that it was almost four o'clock. Twice a week at that time we had a sked with Murray to let him know that we were okay. He passed on messages and information including bookings for radio interviews and school link-ups. After we'd established the Sat B connection the quality of our calls to Australia was excellent. Many people were caught by surprise when they heard our voices – they said it sounded as if we were ringing from around the corner, not the ends of the earth. Often there was a two second time lag which took a bit of getting used to. Initially we forgot and kept talking over the top of everyone and it became very confusing. Jim and I were both able to participate in a call by switching the phone to speaker. That meant that neither of us felt left out. When doing a radio interview, however, we had to revert to the usual mode because the speaker produced an echo effect.

Thanks to our limited power supply we could only turn our phone on long enough to make our calls or to download or send information via the Internet. We missed having friends ring us on the spur of the moment, but consoled ourselves with the knowledge that at least we could ring them from time to time – unlike the first expedition to Cape Denison. Mawson's team were totally cut off from the world for over twelve months. It took them many attempts before they could get their radio going and begin to transmit Morse code messages to Australia via Macquarie Island. I was very glad that I didn't have to rely on Morse code like Mawson, or my conversations would have been even briefer!

Our communications went directly into the international system through a network of satellites owned and operated by INMARSAT. Fortunately modern technology has made communication possible to and from areas of the world where other telecommunications are poor, unreliable or simply nonexistent. Cape Denison is on the edge of the satellite 'footprint' and once the satellite link was made the operation was similar to that of our telephone at home. When I sent my first couple of magazine articles through to *New Idea*, along with our diary for my school to Vic Ed, I was thrilled to receive almost immediate advice that they had arrived safely in the 'real world'.

I had no appreciation, so early in the year, just how important modern technology was going to be in our lives. It would become an emotional lifeline for us as the weather and darkness began rapidly closing in. With the sea ice growing outwards into the Southern Ocean and forming a solid barrier around the continent, we would often feel as alone and isolated as if we were living on another planet.

But for now, I had to think about getting dinner.

8.

'Does Your Sneeze Freeze?'

*T*he 30th of March was the day the last penguin alive on Cape Denison left us and headed for the open sea. He'd pushed his luck a bit by hanging around and was fortunate to have escaped so long after the rest of the population had already headed for the pack ice. On the day he left, ice was again forming across Commonwealth Bay, so rather than swimming away like his friends he had to walk out. Quite a journey across all that rough ice! The last thing we saw of him was a little black dot waddling out determinedly past the first island and disappearing across the frozen sea.

Jim and I stood at the door of our hut watching him go. We were jubilant that one more Adelie had survived his moult and escaped the continent, but at the same time we felt empty because it meant that essentially we were alone for the next eight months or so. We expected to see the odd hardy seal for a few more weeks yet, but the little black and white clowns of Cape Denison had gone and we felt abandoned.

We geared up heavily against the cold wind and bleak sky and wandered around checking that we hadn't overlooked any birds in our regular 'stocktakes' – verifying, I guess, that we really were alone. Standing high up on Azimuth Hill, with the wind buffeting me, I struggled to keep my footing as I pivoted 360 degrees. I did this spin-on-the-spot regularly, endeavouring to take in everything around me. A simple glance in one direction was never enough; turning full circle allowed me to admire the landscape of my Antarctic backyard, and to absorb and think about our changing circumstances.

Most of the thousands of penguin nesting sites were covered with various layers of snow, but the bile-green excreta and tufts of recently shed fluffy down betrayed the spots where the last groups had spent their final days on land. To my eyes the landscape had become more desolate and empty now that Adelies were no longer sharing our home paddock with us. The few petrels circling overhead would be thinking about warmer climates too and I began to ponder the perilous journey they had ahead of them.

The journeys of Drake, Cook and other legendary sailors are read about and recalled with awe and amazement, but what about the efforts of the little Wilson storm petrels? They weigh only a few grams and yet fly halfway around the world each autumn and spring. How do these little creatures find their way? Where do they get the stamina and endurance to complete such journeys? This filled me with awe as I watched them gracefully skim and glide over Commonwealth Bay.

Migration is said to have evolved to enable a species to survive. Petrels fly to more favourable places when conditions in Antarctica become too harsh. This is an instinctive behaviour and not something they learn from experience. I wondered how the birds inhabiting Cape Denison know it is time to migrate. The temperature and general deterioration in weather must help to indicate departure day. Perhaps the changing duration of daylight stimulates their 'departure senses' too.

Not all petrels survive the journey to far-off lands — hazards along the way eliminate the weak. But it's an amazing phenomenon and one that would have me searching the skies in late September and early October for the safe return of our little feathered friends.

I glanced across at the beautiful bay. The surface was choked with brash ice and small ice floes were forming. Further out towards the horizon the large bergs formed silhouettes of icy pinnacles and contorted shapes and appeared locked into place by the thick sea ice forming around their base. The ice ledges along the rocky coast of the Cape were growing outwards almost daily. From my position high above the scene they looked like wide white margins, outlining and accentuating every squiggle and bump between Antarctica's own Land's End and John O'Groats, to the east and west of Cape Denison.

As I stood there trying to take in the scene I was frustrated at not being able to find words or phrases adequate to describe what I saw. Then I remembered listening to an interview on the radio in which an English scientist attempted to share his experience of Antarctica. He said that the best way to understand it was to choose your favourite piece of music, the one that makes you go all goosepimply, and then put yourself into a freezing white room with the music turned up full blast. That, he said, is how Antarctica feels. It's like music through your eyes, and nothing can prepare you for how loud the scenery is down there!

The wind that had been brisk and refreshing only minutes before had begun to gather speed and was becoming more a deadly enemy.

The blasts of frigid air searched busily for chinks in my Gore-Tex clothing, and I was eager to return to the security of the hut. Jim leaned towards me so that his mouth was next to my ear and tried shouting something. His voice was cut off at the mouth, so without further attempts to speak we climbed down over the boulders as nimbly as we could. Shaking our hands vigorously to return some warmth to them we trudged home feeling more alone than ever before in our lives.

Our website was launched at the beginning of the school year and was already being visited by many classes throughout Australia. Students and teachers were leaving us brief messages in the electronic Guestbook, often asking questions too. Jim and I had lots of fun sending replies and would spend hours at our computers each week corresponding with everyone. Some long-lost friends began making contact with us through the website also and it was a real thrill to find their messages. We even heard from some of our relatives in Britain that we had never met before. They had heard of our Internet access from Mum and wanted to wish us well.

Before sailing away from home Jim and I were both worried about leaving Mum behind, concerned that she would miss us and feel lonely. Although she has lots of children and grandchildren to keep her company, we thought that the year would still pass slowly for her. We needn't have worried because the reverse was actually true – she was more involved with more people than she had been in a long time. She was like a self-appointed president of our fan club and made it her mission to keep everyone informed about us and what we were up to. She clipped and photocopied all our newspaper and magazine articles and mailed them to family members overseas. She memorised our e-mail and website addresses and passed them on to anyone who happened to mention our names in conversation. Some of our friends kept in regular contact with her and she began speaking of them as members of the family. I think that Mum was enjoying Expedition Antarctica as much as we were, but without having to deal with the cold toes.

And cold toes were a real problem! Jim and I hadn't been able to find a way to keep them warm apart from stomping around outside. In the hut we wore two layers of socks and a pair of sheepskin boots, but the inactivity slowed down our circulation and our feet often ached with the cold. It didn't take long to discover that the coldest area in the hut was at floor level, but when I tucked a thermometer under the table one day and saw that it was minus 21°C with the heater on, I understood why we were so uncomfortable.

Jiggling our feet around, running on the spot or simply trying to massage some warmth into them didn't help. Chilblains began to appear, aching during the day and itching intensely at night as the sleeping bag warmed up. Alan Parker sent me an e-mail describing an old wives' tale he'd heard. He said that wine takes the itch out of chilblains. Jim and I couldn't decide whether we should apply the wine or drink it. Jim thought that both might work: first drink the wine and then apply it by peeing on the chilblain. I wasn't too impressed with that suggestion. I thought I would just drink the wine and scratch.

Chilblains are a nuisance but not dangerous to health. I became very concerned, however, when Jim examined his feet after a bird-bath and said: 'Hey, I think I've got some frostbite on my toes.' The black patches underneath three of his toes, which we had taken for bruising six weeks ago, were still there and had begun to dry and wrinkle. I located our book on cold injuries and together we read about the varying degrees of frostbite. After comparing Jim's toes with the description and accompanying photos I was convinced that he had only mild frostbite and that his toes weren't going to drop off. We read that they would crack and shed the discoloured skin, but nothing more serious than that. The worry was that Jim could incur such an injury without knowing – he had yet to learn the fine line between toes that were 'bloody cold' and toes that were 'dangerously cold'.

We began spending more and more time hidden away in our little hut. The autumn blizzards gained not only in ferocity but also in length. They had to be endured, preferably with good humour, but they were wearing me down. I'd gone to Antarctica expecting the ultimate in outdoor adventure but was spending more time inside than ever before. I was beginning to feel like a caged tiger and even found myself pacing up and down restlessly like one. Mind you, I couldn't gain much satisfaction from that as I could only take two steps one way before reaching the door, then had to turn around and take two back to the table.

'It wouldn't be so bad if I could see outside,' I often complained to Jim. 'If I can't be out there I'd love to at least watch the blizzards rage across the Cape.' The heavily ice-encrusted windows were useless for anything other than allowing some daylight to filter through. Occasionally I would 'blowtorch' the windows clear only to find that the drift blowing around was so thick that I couldn't see beyond the guy-wires anyway. Then minutes later the glass and metal frame of the window would frost over again, and within a couple of hours another icy buildup had begun.

Our frustration at the extra time spent indoors was exacerbated by problems associated with decreasing temperatures in the hut. We ran our little kero heater for hours every day, but there was no mistaking that the average temperature was dropping nearly as fast as the air temperature outside. Apart from our own discomfort, which could vary between mild and extreme on any one day, many things we relied on were suffering too. Our computers were slow to start up and operate. The electric leads were growing brittle and hard to straighten out. Batteries would not accept a full charge, then seemed to discharge too rapidly. We found that we would get a low reading on our cold computer batteries; after warming them on the heater the reading would increase as much as 70 per cent.

Our CDs, an important source of entertainment, frosted over when removed from their cases and kept stopping in mid-track. The tap on the water barrel was often clogged with a solid core of ice and required pampering in front of the heater before we could get it to open. Our hands stuck to the metal door handles and Jim resorted to covering the handles with closed cell foam scraps. The pages of our books and magazines became damp and froze together frequently, even though each publication was enclosed in a plastic pouch.

My hair conditioner and face creams had all frozen solid, the sorbolene handcream being the only moisturiser still useable. The biggest disaster of all was the discovery that four of our precious five cans of Coke, gifts from the crew of *Spirit*, had exploded in the cold and leaked all over the shelf. Jim labelled the last surviving can 'Midwinter's day' and placed it in priority position on the shelf above the heater.

Even poor little Burwood, my teddy bear, was feeling the cold. One morning he woke up in his usual spot, sitting on top of my emergency pack, to find that his fur had stuck to the wall behind him. It was so cold in the hut overnight that he had frozen to the wall. On that same day Jim was doing some minor repairs around the hut, and without thinking popped a screw into his mouth as he needed both hands to tighten a bolt. The screw was so cold that it stuck to his tongue.

'Real nights' were returning to our piece of Antarctica. Where the summer nights had been spacious and spectacular, with numberless stars crowding the twilight skies, by early April we were draped in deep darkness for 14 hours a day. The stars were now frequently obliterated by blizzards, but when the air was clear the sky was filled with millions of twinkling lights from one horizon to the other. It was wonderful to stand out in the crispy cold night air and gasp in delight at the stars, the constellations and even the world turning slowly on its axis. It seemed easy to reach up and grab a handful of the tiny stars. At times like that I felt the universe was ours.

I was amazed that in the ten weeks since arriving on Cape Denison, when we revelled in the 'land of the midnight sun', our days had diminished to a brief ten hours. According to our calculations, every week the nights would be an hour longer. We felt as though we were suddenly racing towards 24 hour darkness. This excited me greatly as it had been my dream to experience an Antarctic winter. I was caught by surprise at how quickly everything was changing around us: each day presented a different face – stronger winds, longer blizzards, colder temperatures and shorter days. That was one of the things I loved about the place, it was so dynamic. We never had the opportunity to adjust to the conditions because in a moment they were changing again.

We had not drawn water from the frozen lakes since the end of February. The last attempt had seen us digging more than a metre down through diamond-hard ice with a mattock without striking any. The beautiful clear water we had been collecting up till then was a bonus, as we had known that we'd be melting snow for most of the year. It was a tedious chore collecting snow each day, no matter what the weather, and melting it in a pot over the stove. One 20 litre bucket of snow could yield up to eight litres of fresh water, depending on how icy the snow was. We were getting by with ten litres of water per day for drinking, cooking and dishwashing. Anything else such as laundry or bathing needed an extra bucket load.

An unexpected side effect of melting snow every day was the change in weather it created inside the hut. The meagre warmth given off by the burner caused the icy buildup on the walls and ceiling to melt, so it began to rain inside. The only way to keep dry was to sit at the table under the raised bed until the stove could be turned off and everything froze up again. Our record mop-up was 100 litres of water and slushy ice in a 24 hour period.

Whenever Jim was cooking he wore on his head a flattened cardboard box he had fashioned to keep him dry. I could barely contain my laughter as he stood at the stove looking ridiculous. Having a meal prepared for me was always a treat and the entertainment value made it priceless.

A game that we used to play on reasonably wind-free nights after we'd undergone a mega-meltdown was 'Guess the Drip'. We would lie in bed and listen for any further drips from the ceiling and take it in turns to identify what each drip was landing on in the dark hut. My hearing is pretty sharp so I was always a champion at the game, until one night when I couldn't work out where one particularly persistent drip was hitting. It turned out to be landing on the side of Jim's head.

Probably the worst effect of a meltdown was a perpetually soggy bed. We got used to wading around in centimetres of water most nights, and being dripped on while cooking, but a squelching mattress was the pits. Every morning we covered our bed with a plastic sheet and stored our bedding in large protective bags, but the foam mattress readily soaked up the water that ran down the walls and soon became waterlogged. Well, icelogged might be a better term because within a very short time the water froze and the mattress became one huge ice block. It froze to the wall and had to be chipped away with a hammer and chisel so that we could occasionally dry it in front of the heater.

The 1st of April was the last day of the school term at home and I found myself thinking about it distractedly all day. I missed having a two week holiday to look forward to and plan for and wondered what my friends would be doing. I usually went on an extended walk, backpacking with my dear friend Bobbie. Last year we'd walked together from Mount Hotham to Mount Bogong, the year before I'd spent a fabulous week climbing at Mount Arapiles with my climbing buddy Kerryn, and the year before that Bobbie and I had been following the wild brumby trails across the northern Mount Kosciusko area. I knew there was going to be no such journey for me this year – I couldn't go anywhere, in fact I was lucky to get out of the hut to empty the dunny bucket some days!

Determined not to let myself feel unhappy, I conceded to twinges of feeling a bit cheated because I didn't expect to be hut-bound so often – not that early in the year. I made myself concentrate on what was happening there and now in that most extraordinary place, rather than what would have been happening if I were at home. I tried to prepare for the long haul ahead of me by breaking the time up into smaller chunks, rather than looking at the full period stretching ahead. As a new month had just begun we were in the second 'time chunk'. February/March was the first, April/May the second, etc. I saw the second chunk as being a time of transition, going from the excitement of the new to something more settled and routine. I couldn't help but wonder what the June/July chunk would be like.

Our e-mails and brief telephone chats back home must have been sending out signals that our moods were beginning to swing. Although we always tried to keep a cheery voice with no whinging, there's no fooling some people. Often someone would send us a particularly lovely letter of support and encouragement, or a funny cartoon or story to make us laugh. We really appreciated the people who went to such lengths to ensure that we didn't feel forgotten or lonely.

When Murray organised a secret link-up with some of the students from my class of '98, I couldn't wipe the smile off my face for days. I was told to turn the phone on at 2pm and to expect a business call from one of our sponsors. I gasped with delight when I heard a chorus of 'Hello Mrs Claypole' down the line. I spoke with every one of the children, and about half of the teachers too who were playing hooky from their classrooms.

I wrote in a letter to Vicky at that time:

The newness and novelty of living in Antarctica has well and truly worn off now and we're starting to get down to it. We're both happy and very much enjoying being together but the reality of our isolation and extraordinary circumstances are starting to become apparent.

It is interesting that we now crave other forms of stimulation and entertainment – someone to visit us and chat, a movie to watch, a newspaper to read, the chance to see some other scenery or something moving.

Life here on Cape Denison is reminiscent of living in a photograph. Apart from the obvious 'pretty as a picture' scenery, it is static, like a frame captured on film. I can stand on the step of Gadget and look around 360 degrees and see absolutely no movement most of the time. There are no animals, no trees or grass to sway, even the waves are still, frozen into shape. It's like looking at an enormous panoramic shot of Cape Denison, except we're in it too.

To add to this visually static environment there is no smell, no colour, and unless the wind is blowing, no sound either.

Neither of us is feeling miserable or depressed, it's just this awareness of what is missing from our lives that we can't compensate for in any way.

Writing my weekly website diaries and *New Idea* articles was something I really enjoyed. Apart from the act of writing, which surprisingly I found very pleasurable, I liked the regular work commitment. After leading a busy and very full life it was hard to suddenly have so much free time. While Jim absolutely revelled in it and loved being able to potter about at will, I function better with defined commitments and some structure to my day. I find then that I can get more done, as the more I do the more I want to do. Too little in my day and apathy sets in and I'm at risk of becoming a couch potato.

I always allocated Mondays for the school's diary and Wednesdays for the magazine. Sunday was initially set aside for answering readers' e-mails, but as my column became more popular and we began receiving up to 40 e-mails a day I spent extra time during the week on the task. Jim answered the bulk of the Guestbook entries and I would help him out when he became too snowed under.

We loved the kids' questions and frequently read them to each other. I enjoyed the simplicity of their curiosity, especially when they asked things like:

> Does your sneeze freeze?
> Can you see the hole in the ozone layer?
> When it's dark all of the time, how will you know when to
>   go to bed?
> How do you stop your undies from freezing?
> Do you miss TV?
> Are you sick of each other yet?

One young girl from country Victoria sent us an all-time classic e-mail that read:

> Hi. I'm nine years old. Is it sometimes hard to put up with
> Jim? I have an older brother called Tom and it's hell putting
> up with him! Do you ever have fights?

'Are we sick of each other yet?' was one of the most commonly asked questions of the year. Funnily, that was one aspect of our year in isolation that didn't worry me. Being married to each other now for 27 years meant that Jim and I knew each other pretty well. Our relationship had great gentleness and depth to it, arguing was never our way of dealing with upsets or frustration. I was, however, under no illusion that our physical closeness and exclusiveness over the twelve months would be testing and that we would have to approach it with bucket-loads of consideration, love and more than a smattering of humour. I don't think that we'd ever talked or laughed so much before, and we were still great mates.

Little niggles were dealt with quickly and immediately. We couldn't afford to let petty things build up into something that would create bad feeling between us. So when Whitney Houston's CD played over and over for hours on end, I subtly hunted out the headphones and asked Jim to wear them every time he listened to her again. That he did happily. But I had to withdraw that request hastily when I discovered that Jim's singing along, without Whitney's accompaniment, was much worse!

I became aware of a change in readers' e-mails over the first few months. At first the messages were brief and friendly and wished us well in our venture. By the time I had written my first dozen articles the letters had become longer and more personal, and many of the readers began sharing aspects of their own lives with me. I was amazed and humbled by the warmth and emotion that poured out of those letters. I spoke to Bunty Avieson (*New Idea*'s editor) about this and she said that everyone at the magazine had noticed it too. She said it was as if the readers felt that they knew me now as a friend and wanted to make the communication two-way. I was genuinely touched. 'You should see the bags of regular mail people have sent to the magazine. We've never had such an enormous response to a column before,' she added.

One of the few luxuries of spending a year in Antarctica had to be the amount of time available for reading. In our 'past life', finding time for recreational reading was difficult. During the school term it was hard enough to get through the entire professional reading required, let alone attempt to get through a novel. But being locked away inside our hut, hiding from the Antarctic blizzards, meant that we had plenty of time to indulge ourselves.

Jim and I took a box of 50 books and 40 CDs down south, many lent to us by friends. We'd asked if they would lend us a favourite book and CD from their collection so that we'd have a small part of them with us for the year. We ended up with an incredibly eclectic assortment, particularly in music where anything from John Denver to Bach to African tribal music could be heard belting forth into the night from our portable CD player.

A typical evening found us sitting up late, totally immersed in our books. They were a great form of escape as we huddled close to the Tilley lamp for light and warmth and transported ourselves away from our uncomfortable surroundings for a few brief hours. There were moments when the light began to sputter and the flame would be resuscitated by one of us frantically pumping the lamp to build up the pressure. Once we had a steady flow of gas, the mantle again glowed brightly. When doing this I often thought of the little boy who e-mailed us from far north Queensland asking if we had a problem with bugs around our lamp at night. I'll bet he thought I was having him on when he read my reply telling him it was too cold in Antarctica for bugs.

Reading wasn't our only source of entertainment – we had a whole crate of stuff to keep ourselves amused. Wanting to take advantage of the vast amount of uncommitted time available, we had included some things that we'd always wanted to do. Jim took a 'teach yourself to draw' manual and lots of pencils, pens and paper. I packed embroidery kits and, luckily, a brand new pair of prescription glasses. We also had a guitar with plenty of self-help instructions. Jim had wanted to take a harmonica, until he realised that his lips would probably stick to the metal mouthpiece once it froze. He settled for some wooden panpipes. We had lots of cards, games, mind puzzles, crosswords, juggling balls and table basketball to keep ourselves happy. We also read to each other, which was one of my favourite evening pastimes.

One of the most popular forms of entertainment for a short period during the year was Monopoly. Jim and I set up a tournament, changed some of the rules and set about trying to financially destroy each other. It often occurred to me during our games just how bizarre it was doing something so normal in such an extraordinary place. I couldn't help but sit back and see in my mind the whole Antarctic continent, with thousands of kilometres of empty frozen wastes and a little hut perched in the dark on a small outcrop of rocks, with a warm light glowing from three tiny windows – and in that hut a man and a woman huddled over a table trying to roll a double to get out of jail and pass Go, so they could collect their $200!

On 10 April the wind gusts had cranked up to 160 km/h by early evening and the hut was being pounded with small rocks and lumps of ice blown down from the ice slope behind. The howling of the wind outside and the screaming in the roof ventilators meant that Jim and I could hold a conversation only by yelling at each other. We gave up on that, along with trying to listen to music, and buried ourselves in our books. During the stronger gusts, which seemed to grab our hut and shake it like a terrier with a bone, we heard a banging noise under the hut. 'Something's loose,' I yelled at Jim, 'we'll have to tie it down or we'll end up in Commonwealth Bay!'

The thought of having to go outside in those conditions wasn't a pleasant one but we couldn't ignore the banging. Whatever it was thrashing around out there would disintegrate with the violent movements. We both pointed at each other and yelled: 'It's your turn to go outside!' Laughing, we geared up carefully, checking to make sure that all layers of clothing were secure. The weather monitor indicated that the windchill factor was minus 60°C as we grabbed our torches and goggles and stepped into the annex. The ferocity of the blizzard was far more obvious there because the structure was flimsier and not as well sealed as the main hut. Little streams of powder-fine drift were infiltrating miniature cracks and holes in the walls, and the floor was centimetres deep in ice.

Jim opened the exterior door and a moving wall of white met us. The air was so dense with airborne ice that it seemed as if we could cut an opening in it. Millions of frozen particles blew in at us as we stepped outside and quickly pulled the door shut. I tried flashing the torch around but the light bounced back, reflecting off the ice-choked air.

Signalling to me to follow him, Jim turned the corner of the hut to locate the source of the banging and immediately felt the full blast of the wind. He staggered at the force of it and stumbled around awkwardly trying to get a better footing on the uneven surface of the ice-covered rocks.

Hanging onto the guy-wires for support, we made our way around the hut and found that the aluminium ladder was the cause of the problem! While I directed the beam of the torch on the trouble spot I tried to help Jim by using my body weight to keep him from being blown off the rocks. With his cumbersome layers of gloves and protective mitts, he then did the best job he could to lash the ladder down more securely.

Back in the annex, having slammed the door against the blizzard, we took a few moments to catch our breath. Still unable to hear each other speak, we shone the torches around to find that everything in the annex was now sitting under a thick coating of drift. When we saw ourselves in the torchlight we cracked up laughing: we looked like two abominable snowmen – our face masks, goggles, hats and storm collars were heavily caked with ice, and more was revealed in less obvious places as we undressed. I discovered days later that the pockets of my jacket were jammed with ice too. How it made its way in there I still can't work out.

Before climbing into bed Jim downloaded the e-mails that we'd forgotten to collect that afternoon. We noticed one from our eldest son Ryan and opened that first. It was fairly short but I could tell that he was feeling emotional. I quickly scanned the text to reassure myself that everything was all right, but I think the only part that registered in my mind was the bit that said: 'We're going to be a mum and dad.'

What a bombshell! Jim and I sat there and stared at each other, stunned. The screaming wind now seemed insignificant. I felt a thousand emotions all at once. My God – that will mean a baby in the family! Ben will be an uncle! Vicky will be a great-aunt – I hope she's got her orthopaedic shoes on lay-by! And best of all, we'll be grandparents!

Then it hit me that the baby would be born while we were still in Antarctica. In fact, we wouldn't get our first cuddle until he or she was nearly three months old. Suddenly I felt a million miles away from home and disappointed that I was to miss out on one of the biggest events in Ryan's life. Jim must have been feeling the same, sitting across the table from me looking into space. Then he jumped up and flung his arms around me, grinning and yelling above the wind: 'I've never slept with a grandmother before!'

We opened a bottle of Bundy rum and located the sole surviving can of Coke that we had put away for our midwinter celebrations. We felt that becoming grandparents topped midwinter any time, and toasted each other loudly. There was no point in ringing the kids while the blizzard was at such a pitch, so we agreed to call the next day.

9.

My Turn to Collect Snow

It was four in the morning when Jim and I were rudely awoken by puffs of fine drift, just like talcum powder, landing on our faces. We could hear that it was a wild and woolly night outside but were still surprised that small bursts of drift had managed to enter the roof ventilator near the bed and blow over us in our sleep. I screwed the cap on the vent in the dark, and since I was up anyway, dashed out to the annex for a quick wee. It was minus 24°C in the annex but squatting there, even in my thermal underwear, it felt a lot colder. Having to bare all set the skin on my bottom and my thighs burning intensely. I could still feel the pain for some time after climbing back into bed and snuggling up close to Jim.

I expected that with the pressure off my bladder, and no more snow in my face, I could settle down for another couple of hours of lovely deep sleep. Wrong! It seemed that the cold was determined to creep through or under the bed covers in any way it could. I lay there hugging myself, with Jim huddled behind me, but I was still freezing. Jim had pulled his hat right down over his eyes to stop his eyeballs from chilling, and his beard was white with frost. I felt as if I was in bed with Santa Claus. The sheet liner in our sleeping bag was damp and crisp around the edges where the condensation from our breath had been absorbed and frozen stiff. The worst part was the icy pillow. It chilled our faces every time we rolled over or moved away from the warm spot where we lay. Jim's pillow had actually frozen to the wall and he was unable to move it at all. Despite suffering all that for hours, it still took a huge burst of willpower to get up and start the day.

It was my turn to get up first and begin the daily routine. With as much determination as I could muster I extricated myself from my down cocoon and crawled across the doona to lower myself onto the table. The step down from the table to the floor was expertly calculated so that my bare feet didn't make contact with the icy boards. My Ugg boots were always meticulously positioned last thing at night so that I could step straight into them while I dressed.

Clean underwear every day and fresh outer garments were a distant memory. What we slept in formed the first layer of our daywear and we piled on top of it the same fleece gear we had been living in since landing on the continent. I never spent a moment wondering what I was going to wear each day. Fashion had no place in Gadget Hut, I just put on everything!

As there was no dirt in our environment we decided to let our smell be the determiner of when our clothes needed washing. Laundering was a marathon task requiring many hours and lots of fuel for melting and heating water; and drying the clothes before they froze was a joke. For days after a washing binge we would have frozen knickers, socks and thermal underwear festooning the hut, stiff as boards, and no closer to being dry than when they were first hung up.

Struggling to put on my three layers of fleece clothing in world record time, I cursed my socks and boots which were stiff from yesterday's frozen sweat. I sloshed the last of the water from the thermos into the plastic sink bowl and washed my face. I tried to pump some moisturiser out of the bottle but it was frozen and useless. I would have to try again later in the day. The weather monitor showed that the hut temperature was only minus 15°C. Because the heater had been off for more than eight hours and the two vents had been open I knew that super-low inside temperatures were inevitable, but minus 15°C I thought was a bit tough. I used to wonder what it would feel like to live in constant low temperatures. Now I knew – it was bloody freezing!

I suspected that I was going to have a job manipulating the lighter, with my very cold hands, to light the heater and the stove. I kept the lighter in my pants pocket during the day and it often responded well to my body warmth by lighting first time. It was a different matter on those freezing mornings when I could flick the wheel until my fingers throbbed and still not strike a flame.

We had decided earlier to hunt out the matches since they would be more effective in the cold. They would be easier to strike a flame and better for warming the priming fluid before lighting the stove. I'd nearly melted my fingernails every time I kept the lighter going for the 20 to 30 seconds it took to warm the metho! So far we hadn't been able to locate the matches and had planned a more systematic search. Persistence of effort paid off this time and I had both the stove and the heater glowing within ten minutes – with all nails intact too.

Thankfully I had filled the kettle before going to bed, as the water barrel had been freezing regularly in the sub-zero hut temperatures. When the contents of the kettle froze too it was often 45 minutes to an hour before we had our first desperate cuppa of the day. I always used that waiting time to do some on-the-spot stretching and exercising. I was appalled at my declining state of fitness and was determined not to let any forced confinement reduce it even further. With Jim still up in bed and out of the way I could wave my arms and legs around in that tiny space without worrying about swatting him in the face or kicking him. It was a great way of warming up too, although all the running on the spot, squats and leg raises never seemed to have much effect on my feet.

The smell of coffee aroused Jim and he swung down off the bunk to join me. The hut temperature had reached 2°C by that time and the place was beginning to feel relatively cosy. Rather than turn the stove off and have to go through the lighting process again, I placed the snow pot on the burner and began making our daily ration of water. I knew that I would have to gear up and go outside and collect snow – it was my turn for that too – because the half-full bucket left over from yesterday wouldn't give us the eight or ten litres of water we needed.

We had come to hate the fumes in the morning. The stove had been burning inefficiently and dangerous carbon monoxide was escaping into the hut, so far in small quantities. Good ventilation was difficult to achieve on blizzardy days – even opening the front door the merest crack covered the floor, generator, toilet bucket and all of our equipment with a thick layer of drift. I now checked the flame and discovered that it was burning yellow, which meant there was CO again.

We had been having problems with the stove heads leaking or burning yellow and were down to our last replacement head already.

We were managing on a single burner and rapidly becoming masters of one-pot meals, mainly Antarctic versions of risotto, curry and chilli dishes. To save being asphyxiated by the toxic fumes I turned off the heater and opened the interior doors in an effort to vent the hut safely. It was pointless running the heater as all warmth was being sucked out into the annex so I switched it off. For the next two hours we wore our down expedition jackets, hats and gloves and watched the thermometer drop rapidly back to sub-zero temperatures.

While I attended the snow pot, keeping it topped up with ice and draining the melt water into the barrel, I began one of our favourite morning routines – opening the envelope from Linda's Morale Booster Box. Linda, who was Jim's secretary before we left Australia, had spent weeks secretly putting together 365 envelopes with letters, jokes, photographs, puzzles, or clippings from newspapers and magazines. She had asked friends to contribute messages and my students to send in stories, poems and drawings. She'd also organised dozens of other little surprises to brighten our days.

Standing beside the stove, I chuckled at the delightfully crude jokes Terry had sent, while Jim opened our diary and found a cute message from Vicky. It always reassured us how quickly the discomforts of the night before could be forgotten when we started the day with the thought of a friend. I would also use that waiting time at the stove to make the first entry of the day in my journal, although I was often delayed by ink that had frozen in the pen. A few minutes on top of the heater usually solved that problem; but sometimes the paper in the journal was so cold that the ballpoint got stuck again and the pen had to be put back on the heater.

Jim's priority for the day was to run the generator for the first time to put a charge into our three large marine batteries. As we headed towards winter the diminishing daylight meant less opportunity for the solar panels to pump the amps we needed into the batteries. And as heavy blizzards were becoming a common feature of our week, the sun was often unable to penetrate the clouds of drift anyway.

We had deliberately engineered things so that none of our survival equipment would rely on electrical power, as it was likely to be one of our most valuable but uncertain commodities. Our stove, which was probably the most vital piece of survival equipment – for its function of making our water – ran on ATK (aviation turbine kerosene). The heater and lamps also ran on ATK, which is a cleaner burning fuel and reasonably efficient in extremely low temperatures. Only our communications equipment and our video cameras needed electric power.

Until recently, with restrained use, we'd been able to run our phone and recharge the computer and camera batteries on solar power alone. Unfortunately those times had passed and we had to use the diesel generator. We had already lugged the three batteries out of the middle room, where they had been sitting in consistently low temperatures, into the warmer living quarters with us. They were placed on the bench close to the heater in the hope that when warm they would accept and hold a charge more readily. Cold batteries perform badly and we were relying on these units to keep us in touch with the rest of the world. The trouble was, our total bench space was halved to only 70 centimetres.

The generator was stored out in the annex and every part of the machine was frozen and too cold to touch with bare hands.

Jim again had a devil of a job getting it started. It didn't help his state of mind when, after pulling the cord at least 20 times, he discovered that he hadn't turned the fuel on! The motor kicked over first time after that. It took only 20 minutes to top up the batteries – and didn't that put a smile back on his face!

However, the generator was to become the bane of Jim's life. First, it became harder and harder to start it up in the extremely cold annex. When Jim pushed open the door into our living quarters one day, dragging the generator behind him, and announced, 'Meet Genny, our new room-mate', I was horrified. She was given my favourite spot, right in front of the heater, and our one metre by one metre floor space was reduced to almost half. Our tiny room, appropriately called a 'shoe box' by the crew at *New Idea*, was becoming hopelessly crowded with hardware. The only consolation was that no more stuff could be brought in, as we had just about run out of space.

The pampering the generator received didn't guarantee smooth running, however, and a series of mechanical and electrical breakdowns began to plague our days. When the alternator finally packed it in Jim was totally frustrated and felt deeply responsible and burdened by the problem. This was the first real low point in his year. I felt absolutely useless and could only offer words of encouragement and cups of tea.

A series of phone calls were organised by Don McIntyre to Mark Coates, a marine electrician in Sydney. These enabled Jim to talk through the problems with an expert and devise new ways to tackle them. During one of the calls Jim was being guided through the steps for rewiring the spare alternator. Not wanting to be left out, I thought

I'd have a chat with Mark too. Somehow my 'sleeper' earring became caught on the receiver and I couldn't escape from it. I got an attack of the giggles at the absurdity of being attached to a satellite phone by the ear. Mark later told Jim that he was impressed that after four months in Antarctica I was still wearing earrings. I wondered if he'd had an image of me in polar fleece and diamanté danglies.

Jim learned a lot about generators and alternators over the dark months, but swore that when he returned to the 'real world' he would never have anything to do with them again. 'I'm going to buy an electric car when I get home,' he said half jokingly. It was a rare occurrence when he could run Genny twice without having to instigate major repairs. Although he had limited spare parts and only basic tools available, the task was always made much worse by having to work in freezing conditions and by torchlight. The things that kept driving him to persist were his manly pride in not wanting to be beaten by a machine and our fear of losing touch with the rest of the world.

Of all the things that got Jim down during our stay on Cape Denison, the saga of the dodgy generator topped them all. He constantly monitored and worried about amps in and amps out, volts and generator running times. He diligently kept records of this data in a generator logbook. As the efficiency of the motor decreased, and the fuel being used to run it increased, we were faced with another dilemma. Were we prepared to sacrifice some of our heat for more generator time, because it appeared that we wouldn't have enough aviation turbine kerosene for both.

But I felt sad when, on one particularly frustrating day, Jim said: 'You know, I can't remember one good reason for coming down here in the first place. If a helicopter arrived out of the blue I'd jump on it and get out of here!'

I wrote in my diary:

> *The alternator let us down again tonight. This was just too much for Jim and I know that he was struggling to deal with his frustration.*
>
> *It's so hard when one of us feels like this because we can't walk away from the other to get our emotions back together. All we can do to claim some space is turn our back or avoid eye contact while we try to grapple with our emotions.*

As always, the pendulum swings. The down times were forgotten when Antarctica eased up a bit and proudly showed off her wonderful beauty. During May the cold, dry atmosphere resulted in some absolutely spectacular skies. From dawn to dusk the sun was travelling in a short, low arc. It rose like a huge ball in the northern sky, barely able to hoist itself above the horizon, then set a couple of hours later in the north-west behind the McKeller Islands. We would see the heavens explode with brilliant colours, from the softest golden tints to the fireiest blood reds, then we'd marvel as the ice reflected the colours of the sky but in more subdued hues, as if washed with a palette of soft watercolours. Jim spent many happy hours capturing those special moments on film, often having to dash inside to warm up body bits before going out again to finish the sequence.

Probably the most spectacular natural phenomenon to be seen in our polar region, and the one that excited me most, was the 'southern lights' – the Aurora Australis. I had been looking forward to seeing my first aurora as much as I had anticipated the sight of the first iceberg on the trip down. Both are strong icons of Antarctica and I had been told that it is impossible to witness an aurora without an overwhelming sense of awe and amazement. I had expected them to be bright and colourful, but found that their beauty lay in their delicacy of light and colour, their transparency and their continuously changing form.

The first aurora was like a large translucent green curtain rippling across the night sky. Successive displays revealed that auroras were all different and could include a variety of shapes and colours. One night as we gazed at the northern horizon we thought we saw the lights of a city in the distance. Realising that that was ridiculous because Hobart was the closest city and its light glimmer was not likely to be visible nearly 3000 km away, we guessed that it must be another auroral show beginning. As we watched expectantly, 'spotlights' began slowly rising high into the sky, followed by larger areas of pale, rippling green light. It was hypnotic and captivated us as we stood at the annex window exclaiming: 'Oh, did you see that?' The cold finally forced us into the warmer living quarters but we ducked out regularly to see what was going on. That light display lasted more than three hours. We felt very privileged to have had our own private showing and were disappointed when the last glowing streaks disappeared from our part of the southern sky.

The end of May heralded the onset of winter and the start of my 45th year. I don't usually like a fuss on my birthday, but this year was one out of the bag. A birthday in the Antarctic deserved indulgence and I basked in the attention. I woke up to a little pile of cards and presents that had been hidden in our luggage last year by family, friends, and children from school. E-mails arrived during the day with birthday wishes and Jim ran the generator to let us have a chat with Ryan, Ben and Bronwyn on the satellite phone.

Jim was in his element preparing a Mexican(ish) feast for the occasion. His creativity was challenged when he had to substitute something dried or canned for the many ingredients we didn't have. When he found a solitary little onion frozen to the wall in the annex it created great excitement, as we hadn't had an onion for months. The poor little rubbery morsel didn't offer much flavour but we relished its addition to the main dish anyway. The meal was superb and we finished it off with two sticks of frozen Darrel Lea liquorice, which was part of Jim's gift for me. I felt very special and spoilt.

The following morning at 6:05 we had an interview with Gareth McCrae of 2KY. We'd spoken with him regularly on his early morning radio program and greatly enjoyed his easy banter and obvious interest in everything we did. I was afraid that we might oversleep the designated time, so Jim suggested that we stay up and go to bed after the interview. To keep ourselves occupied until then we read to each other, read to ourselves, did exercises, ate and talked. The winds blew madly outside in the murky gloom and we watched the drift blow past the window. It seemed as if we were in an aeroplane passing through a cloud. Jim ran the generator again to ensure that enough power was available for the phone call. The machine had not been running well and the smell of burning rubber filled the hut. Jim was obviously concerned and yelled over the sound of the motor: 'The alternator's only just hanging on. It's putting ten amps into the batteries instead of forty. I can't guarantee we'll get a full charge before the belt shreds!' I

Meeting with Don McIntyre and the crew of *Spirit of Sydney* in the lounge of the Royal Hobart Yacht Club.

Our plastic-wrapped food boxes and equipment were all numbered consecutively to ensure none were left behind.

Would it all fit?

Spirit's crew.
Back row: Guy, Ian,
me, Steve.
Front row: Jerry, Jim,
Andy, Skipper Dave,
John, Harry.

Eric Krista

Day six, and the T-shirts
and shorts were just a
memory.

Jim was thrilled to
be at sea again.
Even the odd dumping
by icy waves didn't
dampen his
enthusiasm.

Adelie penguins watched as the yacht motored into Boat Harbour.

Not all the locals were pleased to see us.

What a wonderful sight – 3177 kilometres from home and Gadget Hut was still securely in place, ready for new tenants.

Our gear was ferried ashore and then hauled 400 metres from Boat Harbour, across the ice flats, to our hut.
The hut's inside space was at a premium, so most of our gear was lashed to the rocks near the western wall.

Last-minute group photos outside Mawson's Hut moments before the crew boarded the yacht to sail back to Australia.

Eric Krista

Our emotions were a mixture of excitement and some trepidation as we watched the last crew members leave the Cape. Our twelve months of isolation were about to begin.

The views from our new backyard of the vast, stark polar landscape were stunning, and the silences profound.

For the first three weeks we collected water from the frozen lakes near our hut. When thickening ice made this impossible, we began melting ice daily on the kerosene stove.

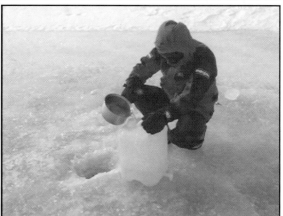

The sudden onset of severe weather took its toll on the moulting penguins.

Ice-capped islands,
icebergs and brash ice
filled the bay.
Winter was arriving
much earlier than we
expected.

Mawson's Hut was
almost buried as the
blizzards raged across
the Cape. To enter
the hut to change
the data chip, we had
to dig a path through
the accumulated drift
to the door.

Large areas inside
the living quarters of
Mawson's Hut were
relatively free of ice.
We were fascinated
by the assortment of
artefacts left behind by
Mawson's expedition.

The Baltic pine cladding of Mawson's Hut is deeply etched from more than 80 years of blizzards.

The wires draped around the interior of the hut connected the sensors to the data logger, which we maintained and monitored for the Australian Museum.

Tin-lined crates hold the frozen remnants of Mawson's food supplies. Jars of mustards and bottles of sauces, with labels still intact, stand on a rough shelf above McLean's bunk.

The remnants of Transit Hut show where Mawson's expedition took their astronomical readings.

Perched on rocks above Lands End we watched the sea-ice form before our eyes.

April 25 (Anzac Day), and our nights were already 16 hours long. Jim began preparing 'Genny' to take over the work of the solar panels.

By mid-May the sun was setting at 2.30 in the afternoon, so our days were only four hours long.

While winds of up to 210 km/h screamed around our hut and 24-hour darkness enveloped us, keeping ourselves entertained and stimulated became increasingly difficult.

Running repairs were a constant chore, as the extreme cold and heavy-duty wear and tear affected the performance and integrity of our equipment and our clothing. Jim's ugg boots just didn't make the distance.

Baking day. This was our weekly bread and muffin ration, until the oven died in September and our cooking options were reduced to only a single kerosene burner.

The temperature in our lean-to storage area dropped as low as -33°C in winter, resulting in fast and frantic trips to the toilet bucket (seen here discreetly hidden beneath an orange garbage bag).

The much dreaded 'bucket run' to empty the frozen contents onto the sea-ice of Commonwealth Bay.

Sub-zero hut temperatures meant that my four pairs of undies became seriously elastic-challenged.

The arrival of spring meant more sunshine and the much-awaited return of the wildlife. With the increase in daylight hours, and fewer blizzards, there were plenty of opportunities to escape outside and play.

The irresistible face of a Weddell seal pup.

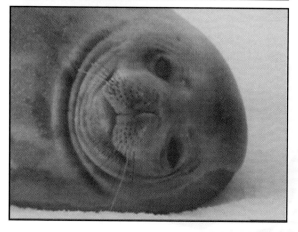

Month-old Alabama newspapers, fresh fruit and cigars – gifts presented to us after the unexpected arrival of a US coastguard helicopter in mid-December.

We were able to send happy-snaps and Christmas greetings to loved ones via the Internet. This one, taken with my very own Antarctic Santa, is my favourite.

We are sailing towards Melbourne, delighting in the warm breezes on our bare faces and legs, and we knew we had arrived in the real world again.

knew that Jim dreaded turning on the genny because he never knew what else would go wrong with it.

He switched on the phone and after five minutes warm-up Radio 2KY rang, right on time. After the usual catch-up chatter, Gareth said that he had a birthday present for me. The unmistakable voice of Vicky singing 'Happy Birthday to You' wafted across the airwaves. Then she said: 'After that, I'm probably now personally responsible for 2KY's lowest ratings of the year – but happy birthday, little big sister.'

What a gorgeous surprise! My best birthday present ever.

It was about this time that disaster struck. We were out of coffee! I could put up with the cold, and even the 20 hour nights, but having no coffee was pushing the hardship level to the limit. For the past three weeks we had been forced to drink tea as no coffee had appeared in our weekly food boxes. When I opened the last box I expected to see a coffee pouch tucked up with the rest of the contents, but only found another 100 tea bags. We had already been forced to ration the coffee as a result of my goof-up in calculations but this was taking decaffeination too far! Just as our withdrawal headaches were beginning to subside another pouch appeared in the next food box. The first cup we hastily brewed was strong and bitter, and had to be the best coffee I ever tasted.

The 18th of June was the first day the sun didn't rise over Cape Denison's horizon. Although we had been living in virtual darkness for many weeks, there had always been a short period when the sun popped over the horizon and gave us a brief burst of daylight. I wondered what it would feel like to live in perpetual darkness. I knew I would miss the red sunsets and tinges of pink on the surface of the ice, but far from being depressed, I was ecstatic. My Antarctic experiences were being fulfilled and I was stoked to be in 24 hour darkness at last.

Jim's Ugg boots were not coping with the Antarctic conditions very well. The soles on both boots came away and started flapping as he walked. Being the resourceful sort, he hunted out the waxed thread, heavy duty needles and sailmakers palm. Within an hour he had sewn the uppers back onto the soles with a neat blanket stitch that his mum would have been proud of.

Not long after, the actual sheepskin on the Ugg boot uppers began to perish and holes appeared in the oddest of places. Once again, out came the needles and thread, but what did we have to patch the boots with? Moments later Jim was cutting the palms out of an old pair of leather gloves and stitching them over the weak spots. It looked as if his Ugg boots had undergone major skin grafts but they did a fine job of keeping his feet warm.

It had been weeks since we'd been able to leave the hut confident of not being blown away. Anything under 110 km/h I knew I could handle if I had to. Jim and I had been competing since our arrival to see who had the best wind-walking technique and could stay vertical in the strongest blows. With his extra 25 kilograms of weight Jim had the edge on me and was always able to take the bigger blasts. His enviable limit was 140 km/h. I often thought that if I could put a couple of bricks in my shoes I would have a better chance.

It already sounded quieter in the hut. No howling, moaning or screaming from the wind (or me!). The relative quiet startled us and we found that we were straining our ears for a sound, any sound, to fill the void. It was so quiet that we could have whispered to each other, but after the need to talk loudly for so long it was hard to break the habit. We both laughed when we realised we were talking at many decibels over what was required. The temperature was on the rise too, so by all indications we were in for an unusual day.

The first task for Jim was to climb on to the hut roof to change the CSIRO monitors. They were due to be swapped over on the first day of the month but the blizzards made it dangerous to attempt to get on the roof. I geared up and told Jim that I was going over to Jubilee Base to collect another supply of toilet rolls – I didn't fancy having to do things the Eskimo way if we ran out. He yelled down to me: 'Take the VHF radio in case the weather turns. I'll want to know where you are if the wind starts up again.' With the radio transceiver in my small backpack, along with a water bottle, whistle, spare gloves and balaclava, snack bar, ice axe and space blanket, I struck out up the southern ice slope. Although the sun wouldn't rise or set on that day, there was enough reflected light in the sky to be able to find my way about easily.

I used to think the cold and the dark would be the elements that would make winter in Antarctica so difficult. I hadn't understood what it would be like living in a climate that was scarcely more than one continuous blizzard, raging for weeks at a time and only pausing long enough to catch its breath. The reality was that I hadn't foreseen such a closing in of our universe and I had to come to terms with that. The hut had largely become our world, and I could now see that the unvarying routine and the monotony setting in were affecting our morale.

It's hard to describe the euphoria that came from the simple pleasure of being able to step outside. Never before had we experienced or even thought about what life would be like if confined indoors. We had always taken for granted that we could step out of our front door at home whenever we wanted to and walk casually to the front fence or down the road. But over the past three months many of our trips had felt like epics – just to get around safely. I regretted the fact that there hadn't been enough opportunities to look around or stand and admire the scenery. It was more often a case of putting our heads down and trying to stay upright while moving forward.

This day was different. I was able to gaze around at will and soak up my beautiful surroundings. I felt that I couldn't absorb it all. Everything deserved a second, third and fourth look, and I wanted to capture it all in my mind to tide me over the next set of blizzards. I stumbled across the little penguin that had frozen to death on the slope behind the hut and been buried under a layer of snow. He was fully exposed again. In fact he seemed to be flying, because the wind had abraded the ice underneath him and he was delicately balanced on a finger of ice attached to his left flipper. I saw footprints leading away from the site. They were the ones that I'd left in the snow the last time I passed that way. They had also been abraded by the wind and were raised on little pedestals above the surface of the ice, like petrified footprints.

I took the long route to Jubilee so that I could visit one of my favourite places on the Cape, the frozen lakes. As I wandered in that direction I noted the drift buildups in the lee of the rocks or chunks of ice protruding from the ground. Although most of the snow that falls on Cape Denison eventually blows away, if a skyscraper were standing in Antarctica long enough it would ultimately be smothered in drift.

Frequently stopping to look around, I noted that the glaciers surrounding the Cape had been calving recently and that Commonwealth Bay was chock-full of icebergs, bergy bits and brash ice. The brilliant white formed a striking contrast to the dark grey areas of open water in the bay. I caught myself looking out across the sea for boats – an unconscious habit, probably from living most of my life on the coast of Australia. I smiled, reminding myself that there was no chance we'd see anyone sail into sight for at least seven months, or maybe much longer.

Round Lake and Long Lake are the closest lakes to Gadget Hut, and sit in two beautiful miniature rocky valleys. We had watched as the season changed and enormous walls of ice began building up around them. The fierce winds that race down from behind the lakes were responsible for carving the ice and producing lovely sculptures. To us they had become a dynamic work of natural art.

Trying to understand why the wind had such an effect on only that area of the Cape, we came to the conclusion that it was due to the particular topography. The rocky mounds on the south side of the lakes interrupt the path of the katabatic winds that come down from the steep ice cap towards Commonwealth Bay. These winds scour the two tiny valleys, carving the solid ice into ravines and creating sweeping frozen waves – waves that were now cresting ten metres above the lake. I made a mental note to suggest to Jim that we go back on the next calm day with our climbing gear to have some fun on the ice walls.

Crossing the shiny blue surface of the lake, which was highly polished by the abrasive action of winds, required all of my concentration. I had only my boot chains for traction and fully expected my feet to slip from under me at any moment. The last time Jim and I walked across the lakes the wind was gusting suddenly and ferociously from the south. To my surprise and delight we were blown across the glassy surface as if we had ice-skates on. I felt like a human windsurfer and had so much fun that I went back and did it again and again. On this day, however, I was just bursting with the euphoria of being in such a special place. I secretly delighted in the fact that no one else would ever see it look the way it did on that day, because tomorrow the landscape would change again.

After stuffing my pack with 14 toilet rolls — enough to last us about three and a half months — I took a shortcut back from Jubilee by cutting across the coastal ridge. The reason I didn't indulge myself with another walk across Long Lake was the threatening low roar I could hear high up on the ice cap behind me. And once I sighted the telltale grey cloud rising from the skyline to the south I knew that another big blow was on the way and that I'd better get moving.

Blasts of stinging drift were penetrating my balaclava before I arrived back at the hut. Jim was halfway through the hut door with the toilet bucket and the rubber mallet that he used for bashing on the upturned bucket to dislodge the frozen mass. I collected the kitchen slops and hastily followed him to the water. The winds were much stronger down there but I felt confident the weight of the bucket would hold me firmly on the ice. It was near brimming and must have weighed close to 20 kilograms. It *had* to be emptied!

The smooth icy section we had to traverse to reach the dumping site was always tricky to cross in a big blow. I paused at the edge of the glistening ice to let a strong gust blow through, then I went for it, thinking that I could reach the blizz line and clip on before the next one came through. As if the wind were playing games with me the lull was shorter than usual and within seconds it felt as though someone had whacked me behind the knees. I went down, the gust persisted, and it pushed me along the ice on my bottom for some metres.

Thinking that I had let go of the bucket I scrambled onto my knees to grab it again. Then I realised that I still held the wire handle firmly in my mitt. It had become detached from the bucket, which was being blown across the smooth ice. The bucket hit a rock, disgorged its contents on the snow and then lifted high in the air and disappeared into the drift blowing out over Commonwealth Bay. Jim was about 20 metres in front of me and saw the whole episode. He couldn't assist me as he was fighting to stay on his feet and hold his bucket too. We didn't think it was prudent to go any further out on the ice ledge – we may have suffered the same fate as the bucket.

Our expedition's aim was for minimal environmental impact on the Cape Denison area and we took that commitment very seriously. Losing a bucket felt like a major disaster. I had allowed a large nondegradable object to litter the pristine waters of Commonwealth Bay and that made us feel awful. When conditions calmed down I planned to search for the bucket, hoping that it had caught on some sea ice in a place where I could reach it. I knew that the patch of ground I had stained and polluted would still be there in a hundred years' time as almost no biological breakdown can occur in Antarctica's extreme cold. I had to do something about it. So the following morning, when the wind eased slightly, I dug up every trace of the fouled snow and ice and disposed of it into the tide cracks along the shore. I searched the sea ice for the missing bucket but never saw it again.

We had no spare large bucket to replace the lost one and resorted to lining a smaller model with an Amcor bag. Unfortunately that would mean more frequent trips to empty it, and much worse weather was to come. Jim also wired the handles securely to the remaining buckets to prevent further upsets.

In any wilderness situation we have found that life is much more comfortable and fun if you are prepared to think creatively and have a go at anything. Problems, both major and minor, crop up on every adventure and they all need to be resolved with determination and a spot of good humour. I can now add 'dental technician' to my list of bush skills. One of Jim's molars didn't stand up to my special crispy bacon one night and a large segment broke off. He was in agony with the exposed nerves screaming every time he breathed in the frigid air. The fact that it was the tooth that had received major reconstruction work prior to our departure annoyed him even more.

Jim located the tubes of temporary filling and warmed them in a mug of hot water, then scoured the hut for appropriate makeshift 'dental tools'. He settled on a bread and butter knife, a plastic electrical tie, a toothpick, a hand mirror and a torch. With no instructions to follow we made it up as we went along. After spitting out plenty of lumps, and swallowing even more, Jim decided that there was a satisfactory seal over the fractured tooth. All that was left was to see how temporary the temporary filling was going to be. There wasn't much left in the tubes, so we hoped the tooth would survive until we arrived back in civilisation. If not, there was always the tube of silicone!

We never located the 24 boxes of matches we were so sure we had packed, but the problem was resolved in an unexpected way.

Jim managed to make 200 long headless matches from the bits of wood he took down for model building. On very cold mornings we dipped a new match into metho and lit it with our gas lighter, which we had begun to sleep with to ensure an easy flame. It all worked brilliantly and meant that the priming fluid on the stove could be thoroughly warmed without us melting our fingernails or burning our fingertips.

By mid-June we had to admit that the quality of our life was on a slow downward spiral. The 24 hour darkness made it seem as though we were living in a cave or underground. We had already experienced a number of very cold snaps with temperatures as low as minus 32°C and wind gusts regularly raging to 160 km/h. I used to say, 'If it has to be cold then it may as well be a record', until I had to get up one morning to a room temperature of minus 18°C! It always startled us how difficult it was to function, let alone concentrate on anything, when parts of our body were so cold they hurt.

We had understood from the start that to achieve our dream we'd have to leave our comfortable and easy lifestyle behind. Antarctica is no more than a frozen wilderness and is so inhospitable that it does not sustain permanent inhabitants, animal or human. We'd known too that we would have to work very hard just to maintain the most basic facilities for survival, and that any physical comforts would be a bonus. But accepting these facts before we left home, and then facing them month after month on Cape Denison, were proving to be two different things. Everything had become repetitive and mundane and our mood was frequently flat. Nothing new, fresh or unexpected was popping up to stimulate us. Our Internet links were becoming unreliable and intermittent as we struggled to generate enough power to match our needs. We felt more alone as we heard fewer voices and received less outside information. How we longed for a newspaper or a magazine, some new and different music to listen to, maybe a movie to watch or an evening in front of the TV, not to mention a meal with no dried or canned ingredients. I worried that we were starting to merely 'get by' in our insular world.

People constantly asked us if we were having fun, and we always replied positively, as much to convince ourselves as them. Being great believers in positive self-talk and behaving happily, even when we're not, we'd got through many tough times before. But now we were openly having a struggle to stay motivated. We were both aware that we had to work hard to stay on top of things. If we gave in to the miseries, the second six months could be a nightmare.

I wondered how Mawson had dealt with things at this stage of his expedition so I began searching through his diaries. I noticed that he reported little on his team's emotional ups and downs. Throughout the entire year he set gruelling work regimes for all his men that didn't lessen even during times of darkness or cruel winter blizzards. Scientific records were maintained all year as well as preparatory work for their sledging trips in the spring. Mawson believed that men needed to be kept busy to keep warm as well as to avoid oppressive gloom. I began to regret that Jim and I didn't have such heavy work commitments to occupy us and challenge our minds.

Ryan sent us an e-mail around this time commenting that he'd noted a change in the tone of our letters. I was shocked by his perceptiveness and at the same time concerned that he was worried about us. I had tried to show no trace of 'the miseries', but when Vicky and Linda also asked whether things were really okay Jim and I decided it was time to stop and have a serious talk about our situation.

While I had to admit to Jim that I wasn't enjoying myself all of the time any more, I truly believed and accepted that it was all part of the deal and normal in our extraordinary circumstances. Jim was a bit surprised when I said: 'I'm not really miserable and I wouldn't consider going home, even if I could. I knew these ups and downs would happen.' I had expected the middle part of the year to be the toughest, and knew that it had to be gone through. I explained to Jim: 'If I could just get outside every day for a bit I'd be much happier – like going for a run. Nothing much would get me down then.' Jim said that if he didn't have the worry of keeping our equipment going he would feel a lot brighter.

But these things couldn't change yet, and when you can't change your circumstances you have to change your mindset. We made a commitment to each other and to ourselves to do more of the things we liked doing, even if it took a huge effort, and to celebrate small achievements and milestones. We began by adding a nip of rum to our coffee in celebration of … well, we'd think of something later.

10.
The Twilight Zone

Midwinter's day was approaching and we couldn't agree on its actual date. My calendar said it was 21 June, but Jim had a strong hunch it was the following day. Jean Meeus's *Astronomical Tables of the Sun, Moon and Planets* indicated that the winter solstice would occur at 5:50am on the 22nd. Jim almost convinced me that I was wrong but my thought processes kept thrashing through his logic, and always ready for a good 'discussion' I began to disagree again. This was our only chance to celebrate midwinter in Antarctica and we wanted to get it right. Who could we call?

Jim had recently rejoined the Astronomical Society of Victoria after several years' absence. He tried to recall a name from the past, someone who would be able to help us. He made a number of satellite phone calls and was able to locate Ian Sullivan, whom Jim had met on one occasion before. It was a Saturday when we rang and Ian was out cleaning up an old house when he answered his mobile phone. He was chuffed at receiving a call from Antarctica out of the blue.

Jim and I wanted to hear the details of where he was and what he was doing as much as he wanted to hear about us. Talking with someone immersed in the sights and smells of an old derelict house in suburban Melbourne excited our senses and sent strong waves of nostalgia through us. It reminded us how we craved relief from our sterile, frozen surroundings. Even a musty old outhouse had unbelievable appeal to our imagination.

Ian confirmed that Jim was correct and that the winter solstice was next Tuesday, the 22nd. Oh well, I was only five hours and fifty minutes out! The roast pork and chocolate mousse would have to wait one more day.

Midwinter's day is the shortest day of the year in the southern hemisphere, and all places inside the Antarctic Circle have a night that lasts 24 hours. It is traditionally a day of celebrating for all expeditioners wintering over on the stations around Antarctica, as the next day the sun begins its slow journey back, and winter is technically halfway through.

We received a number of congratulatory e-mails from those in more comfortable circumstances. Sue Harrison, a friend from school who is never slow in finding a good reason to celebrate anything, told me that she was planning to celebrate the winter solstice with her family on the weekend and that they would have a drink for me. I sent them all an e-mail greeting on the Saturday night and suggested they turn the lights off and crank up the air-conditioning before having that drink. Don and Margie McIntyre, who don't drink, said that they would put their hands in the freezer and then toast us in chocolate.

The first explorers began the tradition of midwinter feasts, present-giving and concerts. In 1911 the men who were with Scott at

Cape Evans had a feast of seal soup, roast beef, Yorkshire pudding, mince pies, raspberry jellies, pineapple custard and champagne. Jim and I weren't planning anything quite as sumptuous as that, particularly the seal soup, but we would be celebrating in fine style.

The weather was surprisingly moderate on the 22nd. The winds were a tolerable 70 km/h, although blowing lots of fine wet drift around. The basic temperature stayed around minus 10°C and Commonwealth Bay was largely ice-free. There was a brief period of twilight in the middle of the day, but the overcast skies and windchill temperature of minus 33°C didn't entice us out. Although not a great day there wasn't a blizzard, and that was always a bonus.

We tidied up, then decorated the hut with our metre-long Aussie flag. Draping it behind Jim's seat reminded us how small our home was. It covered nearly half an entire wall. The table was cleared of accumulated junk and set with a tablecloth and wrought iron candelabra. It didn't matter that the elegant long red tapered candles had Father Christmas faces on them, we just congratulated ourselves on our practicality, as we planned to use them for our Christmas dinner setting too.

The pork roast, dug out of the meat cave five days before and still not thawed properly, went into the oven at 7pm and we dined at 9:15. The fumes from the oven as we baked our bread and roast meat were lethal. Once again we were forced to open the doors and vents. This time we had to open the front annex door too, despite the huge amounts of drift that blew in over everything. My eyes stung and watered for a couple of hours and I had to question whether it was worth it.

The wine was chilled, too well chilled in fact, and the first sip took our breath away. The crackling crackled and the dried vegetables tasted much better than usual. We videoed our gift-giving. I presented Jim with a bundle of three comics: *Phantom* (his favourite as a kid), *Superman* and *Archie*. I received a bottle of aloe vera bodywash with an assurance from Jim that no criticism was intended. When we played the segment back on the camera we were surprised at our unkempt appearance. Hiding under a hat for so long meant that we hadn't noticed how long and untidy our hair had grown. 'We look like a couple of mad men from the mountains,' I told Jim. 'I'll make an appointment for a shampoo and trim tomorrow.'

Ever since I was little I had wanted to do this – to spend winter in Antarctica. And to have reached midwinter's day was very special and emotional for me. I had read with envy the adventures of Mawson, Scott and Shackleton. I'd even envied the experiences of modern-day scientists on the comfortable official bases. Well, now my dream was being fulfilled. Nonetheless, in the depths of a hard winter, I often thought of Huckleberry Finn's words: 'I'm glad that I did this – partly because it was well worth it, and chiefly because I will never have to do it again.'

I wrote in my diary on 5 July:

The blizzard that began yesterday morning worked itself up into a frenzy by the time we went to bed at 2am. We couldn't hear each other unless we yelled because the wind was screaming around the hut, making normal conversation impossible. We gave up trying and lay there listening to the ice and stones being blown against the walls.

It was difficult to relax as we were alarmed by the degree of rocking and lurching as Gadget shifted on her foundations with the bigger gusts. Our ears were not only being affronted by the constant screaming and roaring of the wind but they also had begun to pop as they would on an aeroplane. The pressure in our almost airtight hut was being affected by the gusts.

The powerful wind gusts that hit the side of the hut made everything inside reverberate. One violent gust was followed moments later by another. We knew that we were being pounded by winds far in excess of anything we had experienced so far, and we wondered what was in store for us. The strongest winds recorded in this area had a velocity of more than 300 km/h. I had no desire to equal that record.

It was a tense time listening to the big gusts racing down from the ice cap. The effect was of a steam train bearing down on us at full speed and we tended to brace ourselves, anticipating the onslaught. The experience of sitting in Gadget Hut, hiding away from the furious elements, was always heightened when surrounded by the darkness of the long Antarctic night. To be able to hear a blizzard and feel the awful force as it pummelled and tore at the hut, but not see anything but blackness beyond the windows, left an unforgettable impression.

Things now began to shake loose inside and crash to the floor. Utensils that were sitting on the bench and plastic bottles on the overhead shelves all came tumbling down. The racket made us feel extremely tense, wondering if Gadget was going to survive intact. We knew that it would be dangerous to go outside and check the hut's anchors, and shining a torch through the tiny windows was pointless as the beam would only reflect off the drift-filled air and dazzle us.

At about 3am a couple of blows of unprecedented force hit us. The impact was such that the walls visibly flexed inwards and the accompanying cracking sound was like a gunshot. My adrenalin was working overtime and I nearly shot out of bed in a state of 'fight or flight'. I thought that the place was going to either fly apart or implode and I didn't want to be caught in bed in my long johns if it did! I knew that Jim was concerned too, but he responded calmly, reassuring me that Gadget had probably taken far worse than this in her five year history. Fortunately, I didn't know much about metal fatigue. In any case, we made the decision to abandon our bed, don our full protective clothing and sit with our emergency packs close by while the screaming fury of the blizzard climaxed.

A quick look at the weather stats the next morning found that the top wind gust during the night was 210 km/h! We were so excited and thrilled by the events of the past twelve hours that we couldn't wait to ring someone and tell them about it. The response to our first call made us realise that it was a stupid, thoughtless thing to do. Rather than sharing our awe, Murray was alarmed and felt greatly concerned about our safety. Whereas Jim and I were flying high at having come through such an awesome experience, he was frightened for us and needed plenty of reassurance. We didn't call anyone else.

The following day the weather was still wicked. The temperatures were in the minus 20s and Commonwealth Bay was hidden under a light mist. We stayed inside and occupied ourselves in answering e-mails for most of the day. By late afternoon the ferocity of the blizzard began to build up again and we wondered if we were going to have a repeat performance of the night before. That was one wind record I was happy to let stand – I had no wish to go through anything stronger. I wasn't sure that Gadget, or we, could withstand it.

But despite the foul weather, in desperation to escape the four walls of the hut I talked Jim into letting me video him out in the blizzard. One of the goals of our expedition was to collect plenty of inside and outside footage every week. The more hours of video images we returned to Australia with, the better chance we had of piecing together an entertaining and informative documentary. We were always trying to find ways to show the concept of 'Antarctic cold' in our video footage so that those who viewed it back home could get a feel for what an Antarctic winter is really like. But filming in extreme temperatures had a multitude of problems.

Well dressed against the wind and cold, and barely able to bend or move, I sat in the lee of some rocks near the hut. I had hoped they would protect me from the elements while I filmed but it was soon obvious that I needn't have bothered. Jim and I had already discussed what we were each to do to get the footage I wanted. We knew that once out in the blizzard there would be times when we would lose sight of each other and voice communication would be impossible.

As planned, Jim fought against the bone-chilling wind to walk towards me while I operated the camera. He had to lean forward at a crazy angle, resting his full weight on the wind, before beginning to attempt to walk. He totally disappeared from sight a number of times as the dense drift shrouded him and seemed to absorb his shape. The fine ice hurling at him, screaming through the air at 150 km/h, made his efforts to repeat the task three times nothing short of heroic. I felt sure that somewhere among all that footage there would be a worthwhile few seconds, and I hoped that the images would graphically convey how fearsome nature can be.

The stronger gusts of wind roaring down on me from behind pounded the back of my head as I filmed. It persisted to the point where I could no longer brace against the force and the front of my head began banging on the eyepiece of the camera. With my goggles raised just long enough to get a better view of what I was filming, my right eye instantly froze shut and thick ice began crusting on my lashes and brows. I persevered, continuing with a wink frozen on my face until I'd finished the segment. Later, back in the warmth of the hut, with the camera drying out over the heater and a steaming mug of hot chocolate in our hands, Jim and I had to agree that it was worth it. We had some great blizz shots to add to our collection.

Emerging from the loud crackling static of our HF radio that night was a news item that grabbed my attention. The words 'breast cancer' and 'South Pole' jumped out at me and I strained my ears against the screaming of the wind to follow what was being said. All I could make out was that there was an American scientist at the South Pole base who had self-diagnosed breast cancer but was unable to be evacuated due to the extreme cold and 24 hour darkness. Predictions were that she might have to wait until October to be flown out.

I was stunned. For the first time in months I had heard the words 'breast cancer'. It hit me like a slap in the face. I had been getting by, ignoring the fact that I had been confronted with my own mortality only a few brief months before, and I wasn't sure that I liked being reminded of it now. Always dressed in layers of bulky clothes, I never saw the flatness on the right side of my chest, so it was easy to pretend that it had never happened. Hearing of another woman's plight in similar extreme circumstances put it right before me again.

It occurred to me that if I hadn't had the optional mammogram on my medical checklist before leaving Australia I may have detected a lump in my breast about now too. That meant that there would have been two women trapped in Antarctica with serious symptoms of breast cancer. Wouldn't the media have had a ball with that story! I couldn't even begin to imagine what a gut-wrenching time it would have been, waiting and worrying, trying not to think about the effects of a seven month delay in receiving treatment. Knowing that early detection is the key to survival, what a frightening and lonely position that woman at the South Pole was in.

Days later I was touched by a stream of e-mails arriving from around the world from people who believed it was me facing the medical emergency at the South Pole. The messages of encouragement and love were wonderful and I shed plenty of tears as I wrote back to each and every one of them to reassure them that I was okay. I hoped that the scientist trapped at the bottom of the world was receiving such support too and was gaining strength from the knowledge that so many of us were thinking of her.

The bitterly cold spell continued mercilessly. I was glad that it was Jim's turn to get out of bed first on the morning the hut temperature dropped to minus 18°C. Outside, the temperature was minus 32°C. What a start to the day! I knew there would be an endless list of extra problems to contend with as a result of the big freeze, and it started when Jim climbed down from the bed and found that his Ugg boots had frozen to the floor.

Cold does strange things. At times we felt as if we were still living in the Ice Age, as our items of equipment, which were built for a more temperate world, required lots of nurturing to perform the tasks they were designed for. Our torches would die suddenly for want of a warm battery. Electric cables threatened to snap after the cold froze them in their coils. The hinges on the doors refused to yield and required a 'tickle' with the blowtorch to encourage them to open.

For the rest of that day, and several days after, our list of difficulties grew. Toes ached with the cold, toothpaste was unsqueezable, sandwich spreads stayed frozen and metal cutlery was untouchable with moist hands. Our telephone handset required gloves just to hold it, the cask of red wine had a frozen bladder, the liquid detergent was no longer liquid and the saucepans had frozen to the shelf.

Many of the canned foods had deteriorated from months in the cold environment, such as the sauce that separated and refused to stick to the baked beans, and the whole potatoes that turned into little grey sponges and had to be individually squeezed before cooking. We gave up bothering with any of the sauces – we just couldn't get them out of the bottles any more. Most amazing of all were the coffee mugs which, when rinsed, formed ice on the outside before I could reach for the tea towel to dry them!

As the days of darkness went on, we started to notice small changes in our behaviour. We began having trouble sleeping, so we stayed up later into the night. As a result we began rising later in the day. Meal times then altered. We could be eating dinner at 12:15am, or breakfast at 4pm. Soon we didn't know what meal we should be eating and when, so we started to skip them. We found that we could only fit two meals in anyway, as we were sleeping so much. I remembered reading that in Antarctica it was more a case of weather and ice setting the schedule rather than clocks or calendars. We found that time was beginning to lose any real proportion and as a consequence of that we were losing our sense of perspective. With no time 'markers' or routine events the days began to merge. Our brains had nothing to hang a memory on and we found that we were often pondering: 'Did we do that yesterday or the day before?'

Keeping appointments for radio interviews and satellite link-ups created enormous problems for us. With no apparent day or night to prompt us, and body clocks we couldn't rely on any more, we had to find a way to make sure that we weren't sleeping or away from the hut at the scheduled time. On days when we were to make contact with the outside world, Jim and I took it in turns to watch the clock obsessively. Sometimes our concentration lapsed or we simply forgot and the appointed time passed unnoticed. It must have frustrated those people back home waiting for us to switch on our phone, but time just didn't have much relevance to our lives any more.

The Tilley lamp became the centre of our universe. We hovered around it like moths to a flame. The light and warmth were very comforting when everything else in our environment felt so black and cold and unfriendly. As well, head torches became permanently fixed to our foreheads. We needed them to find our way about and to locate things in the hut. We would automatically reach up to switch our torch on when we required light, whether we were wearing the torch or not. I used to laugh at Jim for this, but I was soon being caught out too. It looked like some secret signal we had for each other, and I hoped that we'd stop doing it before we sailed home. People thought we were odd enough already.

The instinct to hibernate was very powerful. Jim was happy to give in to it, but I fought desperately and made myself unhappy. It didn't feel right to me. My biological rhythm was out of sync and no matter how disciplined I tried to be I couldn't maintain a normal routine. It was important to me to have each day organised and when I felt I'd lost that my feelings of achievement began to disappear. I felt like a sloth and hated it. At the end of each day I often couldn't think of anything I had accomplished.

Small tasks started to become herculean. We were consumed by thinking about what we were going to do, organising it and then carrying it out. We took it in turns to do things while the other watched. We were never both busy at the same time – our confined space restricted us too much, and what was the rush for anyway? Preparing and eating breakfast could easily take an hour and a half, and a load of washing five hours. We never did two things at once, such as lighting the stove *and* the Tilley lamp. We only ever did one at a time, as it was too easy to get muddled. I had to use strategies like writing the dates on each dose of my medication so that I could keep track of what I had taken, or making entries in my journal in order to know later that something had happened that day.

Jim and I began to joke that we had 'Antarctic Alzheimers' disease every time we forgot something or muddled up something else through poor concentration. The trouble is, I didn't think it was funny, it frustrated the hell out of me! Whenever I read e-mails from friends describing how busy their lives were I envied them and worried that I wouldn't be able to fire up again or fit back in when I got home.

When the sun shone briefly for the first time, in mid-July, I felt reborn. The instant change in my enthusiasm and energy astonished me and made me realise that I would again become the person I was before the months of winter darkness. I wrote in my diary:

> *The sun is back!!!*
>
> *A definite sun showing above the horizon today, not just reflected light. I'm surprised at how different real daylight is. We have become used to living in darkness and twilight and I had forgotten how clear and bright sunlight is.*
>
> *Everything looks so beautiful! Although there is no warmth emanating from the sun I feel warmer just by having a slice of real daylight. It's such a warm, happy feeling.*

On the first day of August, while we sat working at our computers on the schools program, we looked up simultaneously. 'Hey, that sounded like a truck going past,' I exclaimed. We laughed at the preposterous idea and Jim said: 'I think we've been living in Antarctica for too long – we're starting to hear things!' But we went out to the annex for a moment and listened anyway. 'It had to be the wind eddying around the hut,' Jim concluded. About five minutes later we heard it again, only this time it didn't sound like a truck but like a plane or a helicopter.

I raced out to the annex again and opened the front door. I was immediately blasted with a great cloud of drift that was not driven by any katabatic wind. Holding on to the door-frame for support and squinting against the blast, I saw a wonderful sight – hovering at eye level, seemingly metres from the door, was a small red and white helicopter with AUSTRALIA painted boldly on the tail. I could make out three occupants peering across at me.

I hung out of the door and began to wave madly. They waved back with rather more reserve. I watched them fly around the hut, not daring to take my eyes off them in case they flew away. As they returned to the front again I grabbed my salopettes and began to pull them on with one hand, all the while waving with the other and shouting out to Jim: 'It's a chopper! I can't believe it, it's a chopper!'

A quick-thinking Jim found the video camera and together we watched in disbelief as the helicopter landed on a nearby ice slope. With its engine still running and its nose pointing into the wind, the helicopter stood on the smooth ice ready for a quick take-off if the gusts began to accelerate. Two young blokes left the pilot at the controls and stumbled towards our hut. I was so excited at seeing real people arrive out of the blue that I wanted to race over and give them both a big bear hug. Instead we settled for a very enthusiastic 'mitt shake' before bundling them into the hut for a chat.

'We're from the Australian Antarctic Division's icebreaker *Aurora Australis*, and being in the area we decided to drop by and see if you wanted anything,' one of them said.

I was speechless. Did we want anything? Were they for real? Where was my list!

Apparently the *Aurora* was doing a winter scientific program in the polynias (areas of open water in icefields) off the Mertz Glacier Tongue, but had been trapped in pack ice for ten days. That meant that they were only 45 kilometres from Commonwealth Bay! The thought of a shipload of people so close was weird when we had begun to believe the world was made up of only Jim, me and patches of rock lichen. And I think both airmen were as excited to see us as we were to see them. We stood around smiling and talking at a million miles an hour.

They told us that everyone on the ship knew about Jim and me living alone on Cape Denison and wanted to know if we had killed each other yet. No one was sure whether we would want visitors to call in and break our isolation, hence the hovering around outside, checking for our reaction. Apparently my energetic waving convinced them that they were welcome. 'We haven't seen anyone for seven months now. You're a highlight of our year,' I assured them.

After less than five minutes they had to go back, as the pilot was concerned about the infamous Commonwealth Bay winds. It was a risky business landing on the Cape at any time, let alone during winter. 'The *Aurora* doesn't have to be back at the edge of the sea ice until the end of the month, so we'll try to get back and bring you some apples,' the second man said. Jim and I grinned at each other – fresh fruit, what an indulgence! Moments later they were gone. We watched until they were just a speck in the sky and then scuttled inside to escape the biting cold. In our excitement we hadn't dressed properly. Jim realised that he'd been out on the ice sheet in his Ugg boots and thermal pants, and I had put Jim's salopettes on by mistake.

We were on a high and could talk about nothing else. I commented on how bizarre our situation must have seemed to those guys – a middle-aged Aussie couple, living all alone on a rocky outcrop on the edge of a frozen Antarctic bay. To us, it no longer seemed extraordinary, as we had been forced to adapt our lifestyle to the conditions. We felt as though we were living on a different planet now. 'Do you think they thought we were nuts, or envied us?' I asked Jim.

We played and replayed the short piece of video that Jim had shot, and wondered about the chances of the helicopter getting back to Cape Denison within the month. While it wasn't certain that the men would be able to return with the fruit, it was wonderful to have something to anticipate.

We both laughed when I revealed that I'd been worried when they came inside in case we smelt, or had left the dunny bucket uncovered, or the hut's odour was bad. There had been no clues in their body language, so either they were perfect gentlemen or everything was okay. Within half an hour of their leaving, the katabatic began to build up again and by early evening a full-blown blizzard was once again raging and obliterating the landscape.

II.

A Couple of Close Calls

*We had found an accursed country. On the
fringe of an unspanned continent we dwelt where
the chill breath of a vast polar wilderness,
quickening to the rushing might of eternal
blizzards, surged to the northern seas.*

Douglas Mawson

The month of August dragged by. Every morning Jim and I would wake up with the thought: 'Will the helicopter get back with our apples today?' The dream of munching on a crisp, juicy piece of fruit sent our taste buds into a frenzy, but we would happily have forfeited the apples for the sake of some company. We tried to keep our hut tidy enough to receive visitors, and rationed our meagre supply of coffee so that we could offer a bit of hospitality.

Throughout the days our ears were tuned in for the sound of an engine. We were more distracted than ever from the tasks at hand, frequently finding ourselves standing at the window gazing out, searching for an approaching chopper. The trouble was, August's weather was proving to be one long blizzard and we had the worst weather of the entire year. No aircraft could withstand the gale force winds or navigate in the near zero visibility that shrouded Cape Denison that month. When one blizzard ended the calm spell was only long enough to allow the katabatic to draw a deep breath and begin blowing again. We foolishly allowed our emotions to ride at the mercy of the continent's mood. As the days slipped by we felt more desperate for the arrival of our visitors. For the first time since our landing in Antarctica, loneliness began to seep in.

The final day of August was a Monday. As if to taunt us, the weather was absolutely glorious – blue skies, sunshine and no wind! We had a scheduled call with ABC Hobart, with whom we did a regular talk-back radio session late in the morning. Jim and I always looked forward to these interviews, as we enjoyed the lighthearted chats with Carol (the producer) before the show, as well as with Chris Wisby and his listeners. This time, however, we were feeling flat. We knew that the *Aurora* must now be at the edge of the pack ice and heading north. We hoped that the call would spark us up and get us going again.

During our chat to Chris on air we told him of our unexpected visitors and our hopes for their return. He said: 'I hate to be the one to give you the bad news but you can forget about the helicopter coming back. I'm looking out of the studio window right now and I can see the *Aurora Australis* berthed at the wharf here in Hobart.'

When he'd signed off I wanted to cry, my disappointment was so deep. Teetering on the brink of tears I collected a box of gear I had prepared ages ago and stumbled outside to take a midday shadow reading. I wanted to be by myself and I needed to do something useful.

Students from Pembroke Secondary College in Victoria had made contact months previously, outlining details of the sundial they were making at school. Through the Internet they were requesting midday readings from all over the world. I was thrilled to be asked to help and kept sending e-mails to let them know that I hadn't forgotten their project but had not yet seen any sun at midday. This was the first day that the sun shone brightly at the right time and it was a great excuse for getting outside and distracting myself. My own shadow kept me company as it followed me along the surface of the ice like a dark ghost. I hoped that my data would not be too late to be of practical use to the students.

For every emotional low there is always a corresponding high. For us, that moment in August came when we were informed that our schools program, 'The Claypoles – Share the Journey', had been nominated, along with 2500 other websites, for the *Australian Financial Review*/Telstra Australia Internet Awards. When Andrew Hocking at Vic Ed sent an e-mail through only days afterwards, bragging that we had actually reached the finals in the educational category, we were ecstatic. The field had been pared down to three and the winners were to be announced at a black tie dinner at the Melbourne Town Hall later in the month.

Andrew, Nikki, Murray, and Graeme Sweatman (the principal of my school) were all planning to attend the function. How Jim and I wished that we could secure weekend passes and turn up too. We felt we were missing out on something very special.

Jim and I were amazed to learn how successful and popular our schools program had become. From our geographical position, so far removed from everything, we could not appreciate the extent of the interest we were generating across the world. We were excited to learn that the website had received 35 000 hits during the month of August – a mighty 59 000 would be reached in the next month. That led us to think about all the people who were connected with our expedition in some way. The number must have been enormous.

We knew that people liked to read about extraordinary people doing something commonplace, but it seemed that equally they loved to read about ordinary people doing something quite extraordinary. So it was a buzz for us to discover that we were sending out messages that not only inspired but also educated people and heightened their respect for the spirit of adventure and the great wilderness of Antarctica.

Learning that in the end 'Share the Journey' hadn't won the award didn't disappoint us in any way. We were intensely proud that the team working on the website were all recognised for their creativity, commitment and hard work. We couldn't have been happier.

Perhaps that's why we dropped our guard and something happened that nearly cost Jim his life. I had read Richard E. Byrd's warning that once you relax too much in Antarctica the 'artificial wall of security you have so painstakingly erected about yourself may give way without warning'. So I should have known better than to allow Jim to go out to collect snow for the pot on a day when the wind was gusting to 180 km/h, the windchill temperature was around minus 70°C, and the air was so thick with drift that we frequently lost sight of the sleds tied beneath the window on the annex wall.

When the empty water barrel couldn't be ignored any longer and Jim began preparing to go outside I grabbed the camera, hoping to get some great footage of him leaving the hut in such weather. I stood at the far end of the annex and filmed as he geared up and fought his way outside. He was completely swallowed up by the storm the instant he stepped through the doorway. To close the door I had to push my entire body weight against it and brace my feet securely against the floor. Even with the bolt in place it rattled and banged angrily as the wind violently pounded against it.

It didn't take Jim long to collect the first bucket-load and return it to the hut. But the second one seemed to take an eternity. I peered out of the annex window but could see nothing, just a wall of white. The drift blew past like clouds of marshmallow, but with the velocity and noise of a steam train. It obscured absolutely everything.

Warning bells went off in my mind. I raced through all the possible reasons why Jim was taking so long to carry out a basic task. I didn't like any of them. Whatever problems were occurring, I knew that he couldn't spend any longer out in those conditions. I prepared to gear up and go after him.

Suddenly something heavy crashed against the door. It opened in a blast of drift and Jim threw himself inside and collapsed on the floor. I hastily stepped over him and forced the door back into place. Then I noticed that he had lost his goggles and that his eyes were frozen shut. His face was crusted with snow, his clothing was sheathed in ice. He still had the bucket tethered to his body harness. The snow shovel was still grasped vice-like in his Gore-Tex mitt. He didn't speak. He just lay on the floor gasping for breath.

I half dragged him into the inner room, wanting to warm him up and find out if he was all right. He whispered, 'I got lost', as I sat him on the floor in front of the heater and started to remove his outer gear. It was some time before the story emerged. He was extremely emotional and needed time to recover himself.

Finally he said that the drift had been suffocatingly thick when he headed out for the second bucket-load and that the wind speed had stepped up a couple of notches. He couldn't find his way to the collection spot again so he decided just to dig where he was. A couple of phenomenal windblasts struck him hard and one knocked him over, rolling him along the ice for some distance. He said he'd thought, 'Stuff it!', and headed back to the hut. But the hut wasn't where he thought it was.

He struggled against the wind for another ten metres and became really concerned when he realised that he must have been moving in the wrong direction. Visibility at that point was nearly zero; although he tried to recognise where he was by looking at the ground for clues he could only just make out the dark blur of his boots, and nothing more.

He went on: 'I began to get really frightened then because I had no idea where I was in relation to the hut. It was impossible to see with the blizzard so thick right up to my face, and all I could hear was the katabatic screaming past me. So I tore my goggles off because they were all iced up and I thought I might be able to see better. But I couldn't hold my eyes open in the wind. The drift felt like needles stabbing my eyeballs and my nostrils started filling up with ice.'

His voice tailed off. Then he said that the only thing he'd been able to think of was to use the wind as a bearing for finding his way back. Knowing that it was blowing from a southerly direction, he believed that by walking into it he would eventually stumble across something recognisable, and also eliminate the possibility of disappearing into Commonwealth Bay. After a few steps it suddenly occurred to him that I would come looking for him. He knew he was nowhere near the place I would expect to find him, and he couldn't bear to think about what might happen to me.

At that moment he tripped over something in the ice. He nearly wept when he realised that it was a fuel drum. He knew exactly where he was now and knew that he could get back to the hut.

Jim's fingers, feet and nose were dangerously cold. He appeared to be in shock. I hugged him tight as he told me that he'd come close to real panic out there. He believed that he could only have lasted another ten minutes; the thought now affected him deeply. He said: 'That's the stuff nightmares are made of.' He looked extremely tired and drawn, and remained quiet and subdued for the rest of the day.

My mind kept wandering to similar horror stories described by others. I had read a piece to Jim only the night before about a fellow who'd stepped out of his tent to feed the huskies and was blown around in a heavy blizzard. He was only metres from the tent but wasn't found for eleven hours. Now we had had our own sobering lesson: Never underestimate the power of Antarctic weather!

Around this time the e-mails we received had begun to arrive in a sporadic fashion. Few people had our direct e-mail address; the bulk of our electronic mail passed through Murray's office computer first. Before leaving Australia Jim had been concerned that we might be inundated with messages during the year and that the flow might need to be controlled so that it didn't jam up the system. So Murray had suggested setting up two e-mail addresses. One would be available to the public and the other one restricted. His role was to redirect the public e-mails to us, as well as forwarding our outgoing messages, in order to keep our Antarctic address a secret.

We loved hearing from our family and friends and from people we didn't know who were reading our *New Idea* column and schools website. Often a simple message would perk us up when we were having a particularly tough day. The trouble was that messages were not being passed on regularly any more. We started to endure days with no e-mails, then a flood would arrive. To Jim and me that was torture. The disappointment of switching on the sat phone and connecting up the computer to find that again no messages had been sent through was affecting our morale deeply.

Friends told us that our mail to them sometimes took up to a week to arrive and that they were wondering what was happening. We asked Murray if he was too busy to manage the mail and offered to make other arrangements. Murray sought to reassure us that he had things under control. We regretted that the administration of Expedition Antarctica had been organised in such a way that it relied heavily on one individual.

Spring arrived in a blaze of calm, sunny weather. As the golden light hit the ice it gave it a warm look that belied the freezing temperature. For Jim and me the day was perfect, a promise of what was to come. We were rapt at having joined the ranks of those who had survived a winter in Antarctica. I sat outside for breakfast, well rugged up, with my bowl of yoghurt and muesli. I wanted to enjoy every moment of such a warm, beautiful spring morning. I also wanted to celebrate the end of winter and the beginning of a glorious new season. When the yoghurt began freezing in the bowl before I could eat it I remembered that warmth was a relative thing.

And we received electronic mail that day. Among it was a photograph sent by Grant, a teacher at my school. It was the staff photo and everyone had adopted the theme of Antarctica. I was delighted to find that the entire gang had dressed up in beanies, jackets, scarves, goggles and gloves. I noticed that Mike had cottonwool snow hanging off his glasses and that Morrie, who hates having her photo taken, had disappeared behind a big black balaclava. I wistfully thought that they looked a whole lot warmer than I had felt in a long time.

With the arrival of spring and the promise of better weather Jim and I were hopeful of a chance to expose parts of our body to fresh air and sunshine. After being hidden beneath layers of clothing since we'd arrived in the Antarctic our skin was showing signs of stress. We frequently developed annoying little patches of dry skin or itchy rashes that came and went all year. But the weirdest change was when we began to turn yellow.

In the middle of winter we'd noticed that our nails had an ugly yellow tinge to them. After some time our skin took on the strange hue too. If we pressed down on our skin the impression left behind was a deep yellow instead of white. It looked as if we were suffering from a liver dysfunction. I suspected that it was associated with either a vitamin A deficiency from the lack of sun or, worse than that, the CO fumes we had been exposed to in the hut. I rang John, our family doctor, and described it to him. He tended to think that the lack of sunlight was responsible and suggested that we sunbake as much as possible. It was minus 22°C the day I rang, so we postponed lying out in the sun in our undies just a bit longer.

The sun was shining more every week and the days were growing longer, but Antarctica was reluctant to slip into spring mode quickly. The bitterly cold temperatures and the powerful gusty winds were still dictating what we could and couldn't do. I wrote in my diary in early September:

> *Feeling anxious to get outside again. I'm beginning to think that we are going to be perpetual prisoners in this hut. The breaks in the weather are weeks apart and so short that they barely provide enough time to accomplish the essentials, let alone the things we'd like to do.*
>
> *It's easy to forget that we are supposed to be having fun down here. Although the wonderful photos we sent to* New Idea *today were a sharp reminder that we are living in a most extraordinary place, and that the good times are VERY good. It's just that we'd like a couple of those good times right now.*

Jim and I knew that things were truly desperate when we finally worked our way through our crate of 50 novels. We had to resort to the ancient trashy novels we had found over at Granholm earlier in the year. When we first sighted the pile of well-read paperbacks tucked away on a shelf in the shelter we laughed raucously at the titles: *The Day of Death*, *Young Ole Devil*, *Loaded Gun*. They were predominantly westerns and spy thrillers, and judging from their covers none were more recent than the late 1960s. But it's funny how things turn out. The old books didn't seem so bad all of a sudden and we became voracious readers of everything we could get our hands on.

Becoming absorbed in a book was always a wonderful means of entertainment and escape, but one night our preoccupation nearly caused a tragedy. I was sitting by the lamp with my feet tucked under me for warmth. The hut was much colder than usual and we were both cocooned in our down duvet jackets, zipped right up to our noses and with the hoods over our heads. Jim had commented earlier that the kero heater had been sputtering for a while and wasn't putting out much warmth. 'It probably needs some maintenance or a new wick,' he now said, barely taking his eyes off the page of his western. I noticed that the lamp wasn't throwing out much light either, so I held my book closer to it. I felt a bit tight around the chest, which I found unsettling but ignored until I became breathless and a little headachey. I wondered if it had anything to do with the air in the hut and tested the air by trying to ignite my lighter. I couldn't get the flame started.

I threw open the doors and immediately the sputtering stopped, the lamp flared brightly, the lighter lit and the tightness around my chest disappeared. We had forgotten that in calm weather the venting system in Gadget Hut didn't work very well, and with very effective seals to keep the weather out the hut virtually became airtight. We had let our guard down once again and failed to be alert to the obvious warning signs of falling oxygen levels. The consequences of a lapse in basic safety checks could be very serious, even fatal. We were lucky that time.

The day our oven finally died sent our spirits into another dip. I wrote in my diary:

I think we can write off the oven for the rest of the year! After all of Jim's work on it over the months, the flame is still burning an ugly yellow. Then to finish it all off we had

an almighty fuel leak! We hurriedly released the pressure in
the canister and extinguished the heater so that we didn't go
up in flames.

When the leak occurred, kero poured down the back of the stove, flooded the bottom of the oven, ran across the crate it stood on onto the cooking pans below, and seeped into the ice on the floor. The problem was that our cleaning-up materials were limited – no newspaper and barely enough paper towel – and we had about a litre of kero to mop up.

The sad consequence of not having an oven meant that there was no more bread for the rest of the year, no anniversary roasts and no Christmas dinner. We had already been severely restricted, with only one stovetop burner operating for the past few months – now it was much worse. My own kitchen at home with its four hotplates, two ovens and a microwave used to seem excessive, but suddenly I found the thought of returning to it extremely appealing. And the very best part to my mind was that there would be no need for messy refuelling, pumping and priming, and there'd be no toxic fumes!

When the last burner on the stovetop also gave up a short time after the oven we were almost philosophical about it. Both the generator and the stove had been a day-by-day proposition for months, relying on Jim's skills, creativity and persistence to keep them operating. Neither our power supply nor our cooking facility were a given at any time. The constant uncertainty was quite stressful as we were always planning the next step 'just in case'. It was almost a relief to reach the end we knew was inevitable, and to have to bring in the emergency paraffin burner.

As September merged into October our mood and energy levels began to lift. We were receiving 13 hours of daylight and the blizzards had started to ease off in ferocity and duration. The temperatures were still bitter but the amount of sunshine to reach us was increasing. Although we didn't feel any more comfortable at least it looked warmer, and that made us happier. The solar panels again began contributing to our store of energy and much to Jim's relief the need to run the generator was diminishing. The effect on our morale was amazing. Our sense of fun returned and we were motivated to get busy again.

One fabulous day that will always stay in my mind was the day we discovered that our sleds were not only handy for hauling gear around but also made great toboggans! Taking advantage of the clear, calm weather we had been carting our stockpile of empty fuel containers and bags of rubbish across to Granholm. In our hurry to get the job done we were shortcutting across the frozen surface of Boat Harbour.

It was on one of those return trips, as we struggled up the ice slope back to the hut, that the potential for a race struck Jim. We dropped our harnesses, removed the rigid traces and propelled ourselves over the lip of the steep slope. With no ability to steer or brake we hurtled down the ice and across the tidal flats at a rate of knots. It was the roughest and fastest toboggan ride I had ever had. With only polished ice to slide across and no snow to slow us down, along with the odd rock to bounce over, it was a precarious but exhilarating course. We wore ourselves out trudging up and sliding down that slope like a couple of kids on a holiday, having more fun than we'd had in a long time.

Since the weather was holding up I wanted to tour the Cape. There were parts that I hadn't seen for months. Among other things I wanted to see if the rookeries were emerging from beneath their blanket of snow, ready to receive the Adelies that would be returning soon. I bet Jim that the first penguin would return on 15 October. He claimed that the 17th would be closer. We based our guesses on the records left by both Mawson and the McIntyres, who had seen the first Adelies arrive around the middle of the month. The loser of the bet had to tow the winner around Boat Harbour in a sled.

We walked the full length and breadth of our backyard, climbing up on to many of the high rocky points and soaking up the spectacular vistas. The ice cliffs were stunning as the sun belted down on them. We could see magnificent bands of blue and 'Peppermint Crisp' green ice shining through in horizontal layers. I had to admit that our feathered friends were blessed with the best views on the continent from their little pebble nests. I just hoped that they wouldn't be too busy with their parenthood roles to appreciate the panorama.

As the early afternoon sun sank low in the sky and the wind began to pick up again we reluctantly walked back along the moraine line towards our own little valley. The fields of crevasses cutting across the ice cap were clearly visible from our high vantage point. We could see that many were gaping open and had been blown clear of all traces of snow. They looked like jagged blue scars on the smooth white surface of the slope.

The sea was frozen, flat and white for as far as we could see. A few large bergs that had calved late last season were solidly grounded beneath the cliffs they had broken away from. They were waiting patiently for the swells and turbulent waves of summer to release them and carry them out into the open ocean. A flock of Antarctic petrels were sleeping tightly together in a group on the sea ice, while a few soared restlessly on the air thermals around the cliff faces.

Jim discovered what appeared to be an ancient penguin burial ground. There were lots of old penguin bodies, all featherless and dried out, seemingly deposited in a depression between large boulders high up on a rocky pinnacle. We chatted all the way home about how long they might have been there and how they got there in the first place. We have since spoken to others about our find and no one could solve the mystery for us.

The fine weather meant that we spent plenty of days outside, with one notable exception – Saturday 25 September. That was the Australian Rules grand-final day in Melbourne and we weren't going to miss out just because we were in Antarctica. Ironically, neither Jim nor I were football fans before leaving home, but throughout winter our shortwave radio often managed to pick up Tim Lane's broadcast on Radio Australia and we became Aussie Rules enthusiasts.

When Tim unexpectedly sent us a greeting over the radio just before the Kangaroos v. Carlton match we really felt involved in the footy finals fever! We later learned that Vicky had rung him during the week to tell him that we would be listening from Cape Denison. The following day was cold, windy and dreary, so we listened to the entire National Rugby League grand final too. I didn't understand much about the game but I sure got a buzz when Melbourne Storm won.

At this stage of the year we were definitely not selective about what we listened to on the radio. Receiving a transmission was always a touch and go affair. A whole host of things such as weather, sunspots and auroras had an effect on the radio waves. Even the state of the sea ice could determine whether we could receive on a given day. After months of monotonous sameness, with little to stimulate or hold our attention, Jim and I would listen to and enjoy anything. The radio offered new voices, opinions, events and ideas. Everything was interesting to us. One night the only broadcast we could clearly hear came from Papua New Guinea and was in Pidgin English. We had no idea what they were saying but we loved the music and the company and listened to the end.

Through our intermittent radio reception we were able to follow some of the world news and the current affairs at home. We knew there were many gaps in what we heard but friends would often fill them in for us in their e-mails and sat phone calls. When a surprise Victorian state election was called I asked Vicky to find out how we could vote. The long and short of her enquiries was that we couldn't. We were shocked. 'Surely there's a facility for electronic voting. This is 1999,' I responded disbelievingly. To cap it all off, on our return to Melbourne we received notice of a fine for 'failing to vote'!

The months of spring provided many surprises as the weather became unsettled and unpredictable. Occasionally we would experience some very un-Antarctic weather in which the temperature would rocket up to around 0°C and the Cape would be blanketed with snow. We always preferred to be outside at those times, not because the weather was so balmy but because the inside of Gadget Hut was awash. As soon as the temperature rose significantly, the ice that encrusted the ceiling, walls and floor of our tiny home began to melt. It was like being inside an old freezer as it defrosted.

I wrote in my diary on 16 October:

With the mild temperatures continuing for a second day we decided to flash up the heater to finish melting the ice off the walls and ceiling. I wanted to try to thaw and dry the mattress, sleeping bag and seat cushions too. Jim had to use the hammer and chisel to separate the frozen mattress and cushions from the wall. The place felt like a sauna once everything began to steam. We stripped down to our thermals to avoid overheating and stood around reading, there was nowhere dry to sit. Meltwater flooded the floor all day. We took it in turns to don the pink dishwashing gloves and Chux Wipe to mop up the freezing water. I dropped my novel on the floor this afternoon and it floated!

Such warm temperatures in Gadget Hut were a rarity, so Jim and I thought it a perfect night for a bath. I hadn't been naked since leaving Tasmania nine months before. In a hut with an ambient temperature of around zero at best, I took my bath in parts, washing and drying each bit of my body thoroughly in the bucket, before covering it and uncovering another part. The humidity created by the meltdown meant that the bathing wasn't as pleasant as I had hoped. And it was the first time I had ever had a bath with my waterproof boots on!

Dressing once more in lovely clean underclothes revealed, to my horror, that one pair of my knickers had finally succumbed to the cold. They had displayed symptoms of becoming elastically challenged as a result of the freeze/thaw conditions, and they had now lost their ability to snap back when stretched. Jim thought it was hysterical and offered all sorts of helpful advice such as making braces for them or wearing them on the outside of my clothes. *He* was secure in the knowledge that the elastic in his jocks was made of much sturdier stuff and would survive the year. My big worry was that I had taken only four pairs of undies to Antarctica with me, which meant that I now had just three pairs (in uncertain condition) for the four months to go!

When Bunty and the crew at *New Idea* found out about my dilemma they fell about laughing. They posted a photo of me in my thermal underwear, holding up my baggy undies, on the front cover of their magazine. Vicky said that everywhere she went in the city that week she saw my daggy underwear screaming out at her from the *New Idea* billboards. I felt sorry for Ryan and Ben, who had to endure their mum airing her laundry in public from every news stand and supermarket checkout in the country. Just as well they've got a great sense of humour! My article that week received a flood of letters from amused and slightly aghast readers. Most sided with my sister Vicky, who said: 'I can't believe you only took four pairs of undies. I'd have taken forty!'

12.

Hints of Summer

The moment I heard the familiar 'squawk, squawk' I knew that the first Adelie penguins had landed and Jim had won another bet!

The weather was overcast and dreary but we didn't hesitate to scoot outside to meet our new neighbours. We'd been waiting so long for P-Day. For us it was not only a declaration that summer was finally on the way; it also signalled the end of our extraordinary isolation. We were no longer completely and utterly alone on our piece of Antarctic shoreline but were about to be joined by masses of Antarctic wildlife, and we couldn't wait!

Dressed snugly, and with a camera and tripod securely tucked under my arm, we headed straight for the nearest shore. We found four very fat Adelies about 150 metres from the hut. Two were waddling off confidently towards the rookeries in the east. They looked as if they had travelled to that spot plenty of times before and knew exactly where they were going. The other two looked less sure and shuffled around on the ice without going anywhere.

We felt certain that others must be landing on the Cape somewhere. We had been told that Adelies arrive in huge numbers once the migration to their nesting grounds begins. Although the wind was very strong our excitement and curiosity couldn't be put aside so we headed further afield. Jim and I were gabbling and laughing idiotically as we tramped around the coast searching for penguins. That was until Jim slipped on the ice near Mawson's Hut and hit his head heavily on some rocks. We paid a bit more attention to how we walked on the slippery surface after that, but we were still absolutely bubbling with happiness and anticipation.

We came upon 17 more penguins, each one a perfect clone of the other. They were standing among the debris of broken ice that had been hurled ashore during the last big storm. All were slick and very fat, indicating that it had been a bountiful winter for those who had survived beyond the pack ice. Their bellies were so rounded that they barely cleared the ground and their little pink feet were only just visible beneath the bulge.

After their epic migratory swim south, none of the birds were in a hurry to tackle the climb up to the rookeries on the ridge behind us. Waddling looked like hard work as they tried to establish their land legs. Watching them move about awkwardly made it difficult to believe that they were such superb swimmers. In the water their feet and stubby tail make a sensational rudder and their flippers can propel them along at incredible speeds. On land, however, travelling upright with their short legs pumping hard, they have the grace and speed of a wind-up toy. Jim and I restrained our desire to bowl over and greet them. Instead we sat on a rock nearby, watching them keenly.

Once they'd rested and preened their feathers into place they formed a single file and began to climb, taking frequent stops for brief rests, when the leader would move back in the ranks and allow someone else to find the way. We lost sight of them as soon as they wound their way among the boulders.

Adelies are always prepared to rough it and they choose open, windswept areas to breed in. The reason is that the wind keeps the sites snow-free and enables the birds to find the pebbles they need to build their little nests. The stony mounds they construct afford the eggs and chicks some protection from the cold. Each bird is most particular about the shape and size of its nest, and competition for pebbles is rife.

I prepared an e-mail for the children at Balnarring Primary School who had specifically requested notification the moment we saw the first penguin. I knew they would be excited to hear the news, but I couldn't send it until the following day because there wasn't enough sun on the solar panels to supply the batteries that powered the phone.

We woke at dawn as we had been doing for some weeks. Dawn was at 3:30am, though, and we weren't motivated to get up. The sun appearing so early and shining brightly through the windows made it hard to get back to sleep again. I pulled my hat down over my face and eventually drifted off. The weather was horrible all day. A classic blizzard was blowing, with temperatures around minus 11°C. I felt sorry for the penguins trying to land on the shores in the storm and wondered if they regretted arriving early.

It wasn't until the afternoon of the following day that we were able to escape to the rookeries again. 'Ours aren't the only footprints around any more,' I pointed out to Jim. Already there were myriad little webbed tracks crisscrossing the snow and heading for the shelter of the rocks and boulders throughout the Cape.

I was delighted to find a thousand or more Adelies in the vicinity of our hut. Penguins were reclaiming the icy shores and rocky ridges of Cape Denison in an amazing display of resilience and determination. Everyone looked busy, scurrying around like little men on a mission. We knew that the numbers of penguins across the Cape would increase significantly over the next few weeks as the Adelies were drawn back to the continent from their winter retreat among the pack ice. Wandering across the ridges, searching out the colonies, we noted that the scene was the same everywhere. The cacophony produced by nest-building penguins was like music to our ears. Our senses were revitalised by the sight, sound and rich smells of each Adelie rookery. It was wonderful to be surrounded by so much vibrant life.

The early arrivals were all male birds. They were quick to commence preparing their nest in readiness for female company. All were busily pinching stones from nearby nests and carrying them one by one to their own site. A lot of the pebbles were still frozen into the ground and not easy to pick up with a pointy beak. Once the females made their entrance they would waste no time in mating, incubating eggs and rearing their chicks. All this had to be accomplished within the short five month period Mother Nature allocated for their breeding cycle.

The mass penguin migration heralded the return of their predators – the skuas. We had already sighted the first one for the season a few days earlier and had watched it glide over the empty rookeries, no doubt scouting for signs of penguin activity. There was no mistaking the skua's large bulky frame and hawklike profile. It perched on a high rocky point nearby and watched Jim and me intently before flying off. We never saw it again, but knew it would be back.

With more penguins washing ashore on every wave, a small group of skuas took up residence in the rocks among them. Having no eggs or chicks under threat, the male Adelies ignored the invaders while getting on with the all-important tasks of putting their nests in order and posturing for the passing females.

The entire Cape rang with the calls of hormonal Adelies. Every hill and ridge hosted thousands of fertile males competing to be noticed. They stood tall, chests puffed out, beaks pointing at the sky, and trumpeted loudly. As the females arrived we saw many waddle unhesitatingly towards a particular male and his nest, where they greeted each other like old friends. The other females cruised among the rookeries as if window-shopping for a mate, taking their time in their selection. I couldn't imagine what their selection criteria were, the males all looked exactly the same to me.

When penguins began partnering up it was obvious that little time could be spared for courtship. Mating took place without too many preliminaries. Then, females being females, the girls attended to the serious business of rearranging the nesting pebbles until they were just right. Jim hung about the rookeries trying to film couples copulating. He looked like a voyeur slinking around, alert for frisky behaviour.

I was curious as to what the skuas were going to survive on until I saw them feeding on last year's dead penguin bodies. Winter had preserved the carcasses well and they provided a ready source of tucker for the birds until a fresher variety of penguin eggs and tasty chicks became available.

Jim and I watched in rapture as the landscape underwent a rapid transformation. Rocks started re-emerging from beneath the ice, revealing lichen growths that spread across their surface. As the snow melted, tiny carpets of moss, so lush and green, were exposed. The warmer days and long hours of sunlight were thawing the ice ledges too and softening the frozen surface of Boat Harbour. Pools of beautiful blue water formed miniature moats around the rocks where the meltwater collected in icy depressions. Much to our delight, some of those rocks turned out to be Wedell seals. Jim had a real affinity with seals and he began visiting them regularly, filming and photographing their behaviour.

'It must be tough in Wedell land,' he announced one day. 'Have a look at the battle scars on this lot.' The latest seal arrivals had bloodied grazes and wounds along their fat, soft bodies. We didn't know whether they'd been inflicted during the recent breeding season, or if some predator had been having a go at them. We had seen no sign of leopard seals or killer whales around our section of Commonwealth Bay but were convinced that they were out there somewhere. When we looked over the rest of the sleeping Wedells we noticed that most of them carried aging scars.

Rising temperatures that ranged closer to minus 10°C than minus 20°C made quantum changes to our lifestyle. We had no need to run the heater much, thus taking the pressure off our dwindling fuel supply. We still suffered from the cold inside, but we were spending less time indoors as a result of the spells of better weather.

The interior of Gadget Hut underwent some massive thaws at this time. We had learned to live with the regular evening 'rain' that drenched us whenever we switched on the stove, but now the entire interior was melting at an unprecedented rate. Water was streaming everywhere. It was even seeping from under the fully saturated foam mattress and running onto the table, bench seats and bookshelves. On the day the wind speed and outside temperature both registered zero we pulled the soggy mattress off the bed, took it outside and tied it to the sloping annex wall in the hope of thawing and drying it out. It had been frozen around the edges and soaking wet for eight months. What a luxury it would be to lie in a dry bed!

As the meltdown progressed we tried to speed up the process by chipping off the thickest ice growths that lined the walls, ceiling, floor and windows. When Jim removed the buildup from the heavily encrusted table window we were surprised at how large it actually was. Since March we had been able only to look through a tiny clear spot in the centre.

Time sped up and the days raced by. The weather could at best be described as unsettled while the transition from winter to summer took place. Temperatures began yo-yoing between minus 17°C and zero. We saw more glorious sunshine and blue skies than we had since we first arrived on the continent. The blizzards continued but they were starting to ease and the air sometimes remained drift-free for days at a time. We loved our newly found freedom and considered every clear day a gift.

Outdoor games were back on the agenda. Toboggan races and mini-golf on the frozen tidal lake became favourite pastimes. Our official opening of the 'Royal Cape Denison Golf Club' was well attended by a bunch of curious penguins and a seal that decided to snooze between the third and fourth holes.

For brief periods Jim and I were able to shed our heavy Gore-Tex jackets and our balaclavas and hats. Being free of just one layer of clothing was tantalising. The day we actually stripped to our undies and lay together on the rocks to sunbake was the ultimate. We didn't last long in the chilly afternoon, maybe ten minutes, but having the sun and fresh air on our skin was ecstasy.

I had a letter from a friend asking if I had let my appearance go while I was away in the wilds. My automatic response was: 'Of course not!' Then I took a good look at myself and decided that the rest of the world wouldn't agree with me. A sponge bath and shampoo in a bucket once a week, no leg wax for ten months, hair that had outgrown its style and colour, and clothing that had been worn for ages could be acceptable only in Antarctica.

As I scrutinised my image in the tiny handmirror I was surprised at what I saw. After ten months of limited grooming I no longer looked like me. I began to realise how hard I must have worked to maintain my 'natural look' in the real world – I'd regularly plucked, loofahed, clipped, trimmed, waxed, coloured, creamed, cleansed, shampooed and conditioned myself. I'd even been known to use makeup. Suddenly I was looking at me in the raw – a much older, drabber and fluffier version of the person who left Australia on 6 January. I could see that I was suffering from terminal frumpishness.

The more I thought about it the more I realised that Jim and I were like a couple of blokes living together. We did the same things, we wore the same clothes and we even smelt the same! I no longer wore my lacy underwear. It had been replaced long ago by practical warm thermals that had since taken on a shape of their own. When I took them off for laundering it looked as though someone with baggy knees and a saggy bum was still in them. I now began dreaming of my first visit to a beauty salon when I returned to civilisation. I'd ask Vicky to book me in for the works – and she'd better warn them that it might take some time.

Jim, on the other hand, didn't look much different. I had been trimming his hair all year but he hadn't allowed me to touch his beard for ages. It was long and thick and showing more than a smattering of grey. I think that he planned to return home looking like an Antarctic explorer. When I told him he looked more like a mule trader I realised that I had been reading too many westerns.

Despite the huge transformations occurring all around the Cape, one small area remained worryingly the same. We had hoped that the ice ledge where we'd been dumping our bucket waste throughout the winter would have broken up and washed away into the sea. Instead the ledge was solid and the 50 or so ghoulish 'ice castles' festooning that section of coastline were all still there.

We despaired when we were notified that the first QANTAS flyover for the season was on the way. This flight carried *New Idea* competition entrants who had won tickets for the flight of a lifetime over Antarctica. *New Idea* and Croydon Travel had run a fabulous writing competition with us for all Australian school children. The prizes covered the best 15 entrants plus one adult to accompany each of them. Knowing that every snap-happy passenger would be photographing from above, some with telescopic lenses, wanting to capture the essence of a pristine polar environment, made us cringe. We were relieved to hear from the flight crew on board that they could only just make out our tiny hut roof and flashing mirror signal – anything smaller apparently blended into the white landscape. It was to be another six weeks before mountainous waves lashed the coast, pulverised the ledge and swept it away.

E-mails arrived from Don McIntyre in November informing us of the preparations that were underway for our return. We were thrilled when three members of the crew also e-mailed to introduce themselves and told us how much they were looking forward to their big adventure. It was anticipated that *Spirit of Sydney* would arrive at Cape Denison between Christmas and New Year. Skipper Dave was hoping to deliver us in Melbourne on 26 January – Australia Day. No guarantees, but that was the plan.

It all seemed to be looming up quickly. We were incredulous that the time had finally arrived when we should be thinking of going home. For so long I had been pushing those thoughts out of my mind in an attempt to not wish my time in Antarctica away. Now it was okay. It was time to begin planning for our departure.

The first thing I did was to compile a shopping list for Vicky. She had offered to arrange to send down anything we wanted, provided it could fit on the yacht. I requested six rolls of packaging tape, four pairs of undies (I had only one decent pair left), some recent family photos, and a few books and magazines. Our friend Andrew Waters, who was part of the pick-up crew, promised us champagne and chocolates, and Don and Margie guaranteed to send down fresh fruit – what more could we possibly want? We were restless with anticipation already!

Packing items we thought we could do without kept us busy during November's lingering bad weather. Sorting through the crates of equipment, I came upon the essential oils I used to burn in an attempt to obliterate odours in the hut. Jim and I must have adapted to Gadget's smell, because we hadn't lit the oil burner for a long time. When I set it going again we were just about knocked out! The fragrance was totally overpowering to our supersensitive noses. It made me wonder how we would react to all the smells waiting for us in the civilised world.

The penguins had smells to cope with too. It was awful to see that many of them had become covered in poop. The warmth of the sun had softened and melted the frozen guano that had built up in the ancient rookeries over countless years. The Adelies, whose nest mounds weren't high enough to rise above it, were lying in the foul mess. Their shiny black and white plumage had lost its gloss and they badly needed a bath. Their beautiful tuxedo fronts were stained and the smells could best be described as 'heady'.

The first eggs of the season appeared a month to the day after the October arrival of the first penguins. A female generally lays two large eggs before handing them over to her partner to begin incubation. None of the penguins will have eaten for weeks and they may have dropped to half of their original weight by this time. The female escapes to the sea first and spends about 10–15 days at sea, swimming and feeding, before temporarily relieving the male of his domestic duty. They then alternate duties for the rest of the 35 day incubation period.

Both parents are very gentle with their eggs and transfer them with the greatest of care when it is time to change sitters. Unfortunately, accidents do happen, and it wasn't uncommon to see a penguin with a cracked egg stuck to its belly feathers. It would look so pathetic and forlorn with the lifeless egg fixed to its front with dried yolk. I had no idea how it got the remnants of the egg off and I always wondered at its partner's reaction on returning to the nest.

While the Adelies were my all-time favourite Antarctic animal, I had also fallen in love with the delicate and beautiful snow petrels the first time I saw these pure white birds gliding gracefully over the waters surrounding the Cape. I enjoyed watching them dip-feeding on the surface of the bay and chasing one another playfully in the skies above us. When they announced their return by fluttering and soaring over the hut I was delighted and raced out to greet them. Jim stumbled on a group of snow petrel nests concealed among piles of boulders and we both became regular visitors to the site. The birds nest in little snow caves excavated between rocks, and their plumage blends in perfectly with their stark white environment. I had read that snow petrels are easily scared off the nest, so we always watched with binoculars from an acceptable distance.

I will always remember November as a month of significant events. The birth of Jasmine Elizabeth Claypole was the first. A very proud and emotional Ryan told us of the arrival of our precious granddaughter the night after she was born. Some time later we received through the Internet a series of photographs of tiny Jasmine taken minutes after she made her way into the world. We cried with happiness and ached for the time when we could hold her in our first cuddle.

Another, rather less emotional, event that filled me with great satisfaction was the removal of the marine batteries from our living quarters. The three monsters had been cohabiting with us since February and were treated like royalty in an effort to coax maximum power from their cells. They claimed half our bench space, they were always first to be protected from the nightly 'hut rain', and they basked beneath a nifty cover designed by Jim to direct most of the heat from the fire on to them. I was sure that if they had been smaller they would have shared our sleeping bag with us at night, along with our stove lighter, almost dry washing, bottle of water, torch and computer batteries.

It was also around this time that we learned that our national speaking tour, which Murray had undertaken to organise and have ready to launch soon after our return, had not been arranged. Murray had suggested the idea of a speaking tour as an extension of our 'Share the Journey' theme and as a way to help pay off our hefty expedition debts. When we heard six weeks before the yacht was due to pick us up that nothing had been organised and that we were going to have to start planning the tour ourselves on our return we were stunned. The consequences of not being able to pay off our debts terrified us. That old familiar knot returned to the pit of my stomach and was to stay there until we were able to return to Australia and take control of our own affairs again.

The ice in Boat Harbour showed signs of breaking up early in December. Large chunks broke away from the entrance and bobbed around on the waves, waiting for the tide to sweep them out into the bay. Powerful waves crashed against the sagging ledges around the harbour and occasional swells washed over the ice, swamping everything within metres. We no longer risked walking across the frozen surface, but happily watched the progress of the ice breaking out. In less than a month's time *Spirit* could be expecting to motor in and moor. The worry was that thousands of tonnes of ice had to shift out before that was possible.

The penguins continued to fascinate and amuse us. The colonies were sprawling outwards across the Cape as still more Adelies took up residence. We spent endless hours among them watching and filming their antics. In a rookery high up on Memorial Hill we found one particularly smug little fellow who had claimed an old wooden crate for his nest. Markings on the side of the box, along with the weathering of the wood, indicated that it was very old and must have blown there from Mawson's Hut.

Pebbles for nest building were soon at a premium, with penguins sneaking around stealing little stones from nearby nests. Sometimes their owners were still sitting on them and fights would ensue. Some resourceful Adelies had incorporated old dry penguin bones, and one had gone as far as to use a mummified chick carcass as building material. It looked cosy but macabre.

My amazement at the tenacity of the penguins grew when I saw two Adelies mountaineering. They were gamely picking their way down a sheer rockface studded with large smooth boulders. I called out to Jim: 'You and I must be wimps! Look, they can do it with no hands, no pitons and no ropes.'

The wily skuas were gorging on penguin eggs left exposed by an inattentive parent. They too were nesting. They didn't actually make a nest but laid their large brown speckled eggs on a flat spot between a couple of larger rocks. They swooped on us aggressively if we accidentally stumbled too close to the site. We soon learned which spots to avoid.

On days of desperate weather we admired the ability of our feathered friends to cope with the elements. Their instinct for survival, combined with their adaptation to the environment, ensured that the populations continued to grow.

The Australian Antarctic Division keep records of bird numbers in the Australian Antarctic Territory. When Jim and I were asked if we would undertake a penguin census, we'd said that we would be happy to. Little did we know what we were in for.

The time for the census was set for the period in which the males were incubating and the females were away from the nest. That meant less birds in the rookeries to count, and best of all, while their mates were away most of the males were sitting quietly on their nests and not waddling about and making it impossible to keep track of. After mapping every rookery across the Cape and adding GPS (Global Positioning System) readings, we were ready to begin. When told that every penguin was to be counted on six separate occasions, we thought the guys back at the Antarctic Division were having fun with us. But they weren't.

Over a period of ten days, in windy, cold conditions that included a four day blizzard, we crisscrossed the length and breadth of Cape Denison and managed to count the Adelies three times each. Our final tallies had slight variations but it appeared that almost 60 000 penguins were sharing our backyard that season.

It was now time to wind up my *New Idea* series and the schools program. As I wrote my farewells and Christmas wishes I felt sad that my regular correspondence was ending. We were still receiving enormous numbers of goodwill messages from followers of our adventure and I was dreading the time when they would cease to arrive. Knowing that so many people were thinking of us throughout the year had always given us a warm feeling and had kept the tendrils of loneliness at bay.

Christmas preparations were underway at home but the festive season hadn't arrived at Cape Denison. There was to be no Chrissie tree, baked lunch or Carols by Candlelight for us, yet we were about to have a white Christmas to remember. Linda offered to send personalised Christmas cards on our behalf to our family and many of our friends, so Jim and I posed for a special photo to send to her via e-mail. Jim put on a Santa hat and we stood before a gorgeous scene of icebergs and a lilac sky. We had to wait until 1am for the sun to be low enough for us to prevent the ice-reflected glare dazzling the camera, but that didn't matter – our body clocks were out of whack again anyway.

Another task was to collect the last few weeks' data from Mawson's Hut. The small solar battery that Jim had set up to power the datalogger when the battery blocks died had worked superbly. It was satisfying knowing that the Museum had been able to receive data for the entire year. Vinod was grateful for our efforts and had arranged to send replacement batteries down on *Spirit*. He was going to attempt to collect another year of readings after we left, but the information would have to be stored in the datalogger until the next expedition to Cape Denison.

We took December's digital footage for Janet Hughes, a job we had been doing since April. She is a conservationist working with the Mawson's Hut Foundation and had requested images showing the changes in drift and ice around the outside of Doug's Place. These she would use in preparing a conservation strategy for the hut. Jim planned to take one more set of shots, just prior to leaving, to finish off the series.

During the wind-up period our commitments were taking less of our time and it was increasingly hard to find anything new or different to interest us. Time slowed and we felt impatient to be leaving. Our thoughts projected into the future and we started focusing on the things that had been missing from our lives. We had lived in a closed and isolated environment for so long and I was ready to be released. I wanted very much to feel clean and warm again. I wanted to be stimulated and challenged physically and mentally in ways that didn't relate to our very survival. And I was desperate to rejoin our family and feel a part of society. The confusing thing was that I started to feel mixed emotions about returning to a world that we had not been part of for a long time.

13.

A Crowd of Ten

itting in our half-empty hut floating on a cloud of fresh fruit, chocolate bars, tubs of yoghurt, month-old Alabama newspapers and much older *Time* magazines, we thought we must have died and gone to Heaven!

We'd always known that 17 December was going to be a special date for us. It marked the eleventh month 'anniversary' of our arrival in Antarctica and it was also our 28th wedding anniversary. But we'd never dreamt that something else might lie in store for us that day, something which was going to make it one of the most memorable days of the year.

An early morning stocktake of our meagre supplies had produced a rather sad festive menu – a powerful chilli con carne with rice and a packet of peanut M&Ms. Jim had hunted out the second last bottle of wine and placed it on the heater to warm up, in view of our unduly low room temperature. The select bottle we'd reserved for the 17th of each month had been an important part of our Antarctic tradition. Every month we'd lingered lovingly over the last drop in the bottle, then burnt a message and date into the cork with the soldering iron (heated in the flame on the stove) and hung the cork from a cord strung above the table. It was very satisfying to know that after tonight's addition the cork collection would almost be complete.

It was also the last day of the school year at home, so I knew that the 400 or so students and teachers at Balnarring Primary School would be in a celebratory mood too. What a lovely feeling that always was for students and teachers alike, knowing that there were five long weeks of summer freedom ahead. I found my thoughts drifting back to school a lot that morning. It all seemed a world away but I enjoyed thinking back nostalgically. I had arranged months before with Graeme Sweatman, the principal, to change my plans for an early return to the classroom, so that I could resume teaching in 2001 instead. This was in order to have the time to continue to 'Share the Journey' on the speaking tour that Jim and I believed Murray was setting up. I was also hoping to write a book and visit schools and *New Idea* readers before finally winding up the project. After all that, I knew, I'd be champing at the bit to get back into a classroom and pick up the threads of a more normal life.

For the first couple of hours of the day Jim and I immersed ourselves in final commitments for our sponsors. Letters, stories, diaries, photos and Christmas greetings were sent across the airwaves around the world. We also sent last e-mails to people who had kept us company during the year by writing regularly. We felt very organised and satisfied with our efforts. To reward ourselves we declared the rest of the day a holiday.

Blue skies, unlimited sunshine and a gentle breeze greeted us as we stepped on to the snow. Our entire backyard was glistening and sparkling beneath the sun's bright rays and the air was full of penguin calls as the Adelies rejoiced with us. This was the Antarctica that was easiest to love. I already felt pangs of regret that, just as summer was surrounding us with her wondrous glory, we were busy planning to leave.

We had traversed the first ice slope, heading across to the colonies on Penguin Knob, when Jim stopped abruptly and said: 'I'm sure I can hear a helicopter.' A few moments later a huge red beast of a machine, with a shark's face painted on the front, roared into sight and passed overhead. We stared at each other in disbelief. Then suddenly we yelled up at the chopper, waved our arms wildly and started running in its direction. The pilot must have seen us, as he wiggled his machine from side to side before zooming away and circling the Cape.

A brilliant red flare then dropped on the ice behind Mawson's Hut, bleeding into the five knot southeasterly – an indicator for the pilot of wind direction and velocity. Jim and I were transfixed, staring at the cloud of iridescent colour trailing on the breeze. We hadn't seen anything as vibrant and wonderful in our monochromatic landscape for a very long time.

The contrasts of the scene immediately struck me. Mawson's sturdy old weathered hut, which had proudly stood at the head of Boat Harbour for nearly 90 years, an icon of the heroic age of Antarctic exploration, was almost overshadowed by the sleek symbol of modern technology hovering above it. The helicopter landed gently on the ice and the engine stopped, bringing quiet and stillness to the Cape again.

My heart was beating madly. I watched every movement of the crew on board preparing for disembarking. It all took a terribly long time and I could scarcely keep my patience in check. Finally the door opened and five men dressed in military-like survival suits climbed down out of the aircraft. One of them walked over to greet us.

The lieutenant commander, after introducing himself as 'Rich, but my friends call me Snake', told us that they were from the US Coast Guard's icebreaker *Polar Star*. It was in the 'local area' on its way from New Zealand to McMurdo Station southeast of us. The icebreaker's main task was forcing a path through the sea ice so that other ships could begin the essential summer resupply of the US base. To our dismay he said that the pack ice was still impenetrable in many places. I wondered again at the chances of *Spirit* getting through in two weeks time.

When we met the rest of the crew we learned that they were on the Cape to carry out repairs on the automatic weather station located about 200 metres behind our hut. They were surprised and not a little shocked to discover two Aussies living alone on what is generally considered an unoccupied stretch of Antarctic coastline. They were amazed at our story and shook their heads in disbelief when we told them that we had been on Cape Denison by ourselves for eleven months.

Snake later called by the hut with a thermos of hot chocolate while the rest of the crew completed repairs on the weather station. Sitting at the table opposite him, listening to his unfamiliar voice talking about things beyond our little world, was very strange. I found that I was distracted by the presence of a person other than Jim. Snake's movements, facial expressions, voice and accent fascinated me. I watched him so intently that I had trouble following his conversation – he said so much and so quickly. I was still thinking about what he had just said when he began talking about something else, and my understanding of the conversation was very disjointed. I was disconcerted that a 20 minute conversation with a stranger could exhaust and confuse me. Our 'Antarctic Alzheimers' joke came to mind and I despaired that maybe it had some substance. Later when I spoke to Jim about it he said that he'd struggled to keep up too.

For a few short hours our entire world was overloaded with stimuli and we didn't know how to deal with it. I hoped that we'd relearn the necessary skills on the journey home with the new crew of the yacht, otherwise people at home would think that we had grown strangely dim.

As Snake was leaving, he asked what we'd missed most. When we both shouted, 'Fresh food and plumbing!', he laughed. 'Well,' he said, 'I can't do anything about the plumbing side of things, but I sure can get some fresh food for you. In fact, I'll deliver it personally.' An hour and a half later, true to his word, 'Hammerhead One' returned to the Cape. In a blur of brilliant red paint and screaming engines it arrived, deposited a large box of goodies on the ice beside Mawson's Hut, and soared out over the sea again.

Aside from the mangoes, apples and other obscenely delicious things we found in the box, we came across the old newspapers and magazines and some hastily scribbled messages of good wishes from the crew of the icebreaker. Someone had topped it all off by throwing in two fat American cigars. They are now treasured souvenirs.

Our links with the real world had begun and at that point I felt that we had reached the beginning of the end of our time in Antarctica. I announced to Jim: 'This is it! All that's left now is to think about packing up.'

Spirit of Sydney departed Hobart on the following day, 18 December. Don's e-mail indicated that everyone on board had found their sea legs and were eager to arrive in Antarctica, but none more than our friend Andrew. He had been planning his own big adventure ever since I told him in 1998 that Don would be looking for crew to sail down and pick Jim and me up. I couldn't wait to see his enormous warm smile and catch up on news from home. In our last phone call with Andrew before he left Melbourne he'd asked what we would order if we could eat anything we wanted. Jim was hungering for pizza and I couldn't think beyond chocolate ice cream. Both were on board the yacht and, fingers crossed, they would survive the trip down with minimal refrigeration.

The entire Cape was now thawing fast. The ice ledges had receded and revealed rocky shores that Jim and I had forgotten existed. Walking along the rocks at the base of the ridges we were delighted by the sounds of gurgling water. The ice between the rocks was melting and forming little rivulets that trickled down to seep beneath the ice. It sounded so lovely, almost musical, and always drew us to it. Seeing something else moving was a feast to our eyes. I felt just as enraptured at seeing those little cascades of meltwater as I had when standing before some of the world's huge and powerful waterfalls.

The population of the rookeries multiplied almost overnight. Penguin eggs were hatching everywhere. Tiny grey chicks caught sight of their perilous world from the safety and comfort of their parents' nests. The pace of life for the adults stepped up a few gears as the race began to feed and nurture their offspring before the autumn blizzards arrived. We were upset to see that some couples were still at the mating and egg-laying stage. Our experience told us that their chicks were likely to be too immature to leave when the bad weather arrived. The chicks' fate was virtually sealed before they had formed in the egg.

By all appearances we were going to have a classic 'white Christmas'. On 24 December it snowed solidly all day, coating everything in a beautiful blanket of white. The Cape looked like a picture-book fairyland. By late afternoon, however, the winds had begun to crank up and a full-on blizzard struck us, the first in weeks. It felt strangely comforting to hear the wind screaming through the hut's vents and the ice pelting the walls. Once again we were cut off from our surroundings and able to see nothing beyond our tiny windows. This was the real Cape Denison, so this was the Christmas I wanted!

Late that night we braved the elements to see if the ice in Boat Harbour had broken out any further in the storm. It felt almost pleasurable being out there in the big wind gusts and the dense drift because the air temperature was no longer bone chilling. The penguins were all bunkered down trying to keep their babies or eggs warm. Many were half buried in deep snow or suffered from ice-encrusted feathers. We passed a skua devouring a tiny fluffy chick. The body was still warm and bleeding as the strong beak ripped it apart. The skua shared the morsel with his mate as she sat on her eggs nearby.

I felt a spark of excitement at the sight of new cracks forming across the frozen harbour and the great chunks of ice breaking up at the entrance. But less than a fifth of it had cleared out and time was running short. The yacht was on its way south and could arrive any time soon. Jim and I had already spent hours talking through possible scenarios, some of which were becoming more realistic as the days raced by. If the yacht arrived and couldn't get in to moor in the harbour, as a last resort we would have to go into evacuation mode. That meant grabbing hand luggage only and leaving from a safe spot on the shore in the rubber inflatable. If the weather allowed we'd motor out to where the yacht was waiting and sail immediately. The crew would then miss their full Antarctic experience and we'd have to abandon all of our expensive equipment. The alternative wasn't appealing, though – I wasn't ready for another year on Cape Denison!

We estimated that the yacht would now be sailing through the 'furious fifties'. I hoped that conditions weren't too rough and that they were making good time. I felt optimistic about the state of the harbour but Jim was still anxious. He wasn't going to relax until the yacht was safely moored and he was shaking Skipper Dave's hand.

Walking around the edge of the harbour soon had us in fits of laughter. The ice had softened to the point where it could no longer take our weight and we crashed unexpectedly through the surface into the stale, nasty, sardine-smelling shallows below. Fortunately Jim didn't follow me as I stumbled and splashed my way along the most unstable route to the safety and dryness of the rocks. My boots were frozen stiff on my return to the hut and were relegated to the annex when Jim complained about the foul fishy smell.

Christmas Day was a mild event in Gadget Hut. Our minds were on the progress of the yacht, our imminent departure and our first HF radio sked with Dave. We did try to distract ourselves by decorating the table area with the piles of presents given us by loved ones the year before. We also blew up the Santa balloons that had appeared in Linda's Morale Booster envelopes over the previous week and we put out the candles and cards. Jim wore his Santa hat all day, really looking the part with his big snowy white beard.

Our first radio sked with *Spirit* at midday received no response. We felt very empty and alone, not to mention awfully disappointed, when we had to sign off at 12:15. Our phone call to our family wasn't very successful either. We had arranged to ring Vicky and Steve's place as Mum and the boys were going to be there for Christmas celebrations and we could chat to all of them at once. Vicky's answering machine greeting was the only response we received to each of our five calls. I left brief messages expressing my disappointment at missing them. Jim and I began to worry that something was wrong, particularly as Mum had been unwell for a number of weeks and had only just left hospital a few days earlier. Much later in the day, to my embarrassment, it dawned on me that I had been calling Vicky's work number by mistake, rather than her home number. The whole family were hanging around the telephone in Melbourne anxiously waiting for our call. They were beginning to worry about us by that time too. When we finally put our call through to the right number our emotions were a mixture of relief and excitement. I smiled at the surprise Vicky would receive when she checked her office voice mail after the holiday break.

Our Christmas dinner was by necessity a modest fare of lentil soup with rice followed by canned plum pudding and custard. I had excavated Mum's Chrissie cake four days earlier, allowing time for it to thaw slowly in the warmth of the hut. It had matured magnificently.

At 6pm on Boxing Day we had our first communication with the yacht. They came over loud and clear but apparently they were unable to receive us well. Dave requested that we try again in two hours. As we signed off we looked at each other and grinned. 'We're going home!' Jim yelled, jumping up and doing a little dance.

Our second call transmitted well and we heard that the yacht was approximately 550 nautical miles out and travelling about 220 miles per day, although Dave expected to slow down as they neared the pack ice. Andrew assured us that the pizza and chocolate ice cream were safe and that my new undies were dry and securely stowed. His voice betrayed his excitement and I knew he was hanging out to get here.

We kept ourselves busy over the following days. There was always gear to pack, the hut to scrub, boxes to varnish and annex walls to weatherproof. We also had mooring lines to prepare and stuff to be hauled over to Granholm for loading on the yacht. Each day more ice floated out of the harbour and our optimism increased.

Daily contact with *Spirit* was a highlight for us. It was great hearing where they were, along with snippets of the gossip on board. Our family had followed the yacht's progress closely through regular e-mails sent by Margie McIntyre. On the 27th we heard that the toilet was no longer working and that they had been forced to bare their bottoms off the back of the boat – at about 350 miles off the coast of Antarctica that had to be a chilly exercise. I encouraged them to keep working on the problem as I was eagerly anticipating substituting our plastic bucket with a porcelain loo. I was also amazed to learn that one crew member had 30 pairs of jocks on board, just in case – that was the equivalent of a nine year supply of underwear for us!

Bath nights became more frequent. The recent discovery that we could draw water from the frozen lake made them easier to organise. Our prime motivation, though, was the fact that cleaner, fresher visitors would be arriving soon. Jim then shocked me by allowing me to cut his hair *and* his beard. He looked like a new man – years younger and more like the Jim I knew and loved. I had a long, bouncy ponytail by then but planned to keep it until I could visit my hairdresser in February.

During one of our bucket baths Jim and I tried to guess our current weight. He had definitely lost plenty and I laughed at his white, hairy chook legs, until I discovered that mine looked the same! I couldn't wax them but I definitely had to get busy with the razor before I could bare them in public. I had succeeded in adding about six kilos to my frame over the year – my Antarctic blubber. I wanted to keep the weight although I didn't like the way it was distributed in pockets around my body. I was keen to get home and reduce the fat in my diet once again and systematically step up my activity level to get myself back in tone.

On 30 December Boat Harbour was clear enough of ice for us to put out the mooring lines in readiness for the yacht's arrival. The boot-shaped section of the harbour was still choked with slabs of ice but when we told Dave about them during our radio sked he wasn't concerned. He felt sure that they would work their way loose and float out to sea. The Wedell seals were a bit put out by the thaw as their preference is to sleep on ice floating close in, and now they were gradually being forced to move to the shore. Seal numbers were high and every day we could expect to find at least 30 of the big, lovable blobs lying around.

On the morning of New Year's Eve I gave Jim the biggest, longest hug yet. We had just heard from Chris Wisby during our ABC Radio interview that he had been in touch with *Spirit* earlier and that she was within 50 nautical miles of Cape Denison. I knew then that it was going to be the last day I would have Jim all to myself. 'We'll probably never ever be this alone again,' I said wistfully.

Dave's estimated time of arrival was 4pm. We sat among the penguins beneath the memorial cross with the VHF radio tuned to the boat's frequency, giving regular wind reports. Soon I gasped with delight at the sight of the tiny yacht appearing over the horizon. I marvelled that she had crossed the Southern Ocean yet again and that the crew were nearly here. Jim and I were going to have plenty of company for New Year's Eve!

To everyone's intense relief the wind was kind and allowed easy motoring in to moor. The dinghy was being towed behind, with Andrew, Chris and Eric on board. *Spirit* looked magnificent as she cruised cautiously into Boat Harbour and I laughed when I saw that the entire crew had Santa hats on to remind us of the festive season. At 6:30 all lines were secure and Jim and I were taken on board to mingle with our crowd of ten.

Amid smiles and hugs, handshakes and laughter, bottles of champagne were brought out along with nibbles saved especially for the occasion. I felt unbelievably happy to see Andrew and Dave again, and to meet the rest of the crew. The excitement in everyone was evident and we were all in party mood. The crew was not all male, Alex being the first woman I had seen since leaving Hobart. When she disappeared below and returned with two gorgeously kitsch 'girlie' plastic champagne flutes I was ecstatic. We toasted each other loudly and proceeded to drink more than our share of the bubbly, as our long, stylish glasses were topped up regularly. For me the flutes were a touching gesture and I loved becoming the second girl on board.

The wine ran dry but the magnificent food didn't. Jim and I were invited below for our first roast dinner in months. The wonderful sensory stimulation of the warmth below deck, the smells of dinner cooking, the sounds of ten other voices all talking at a million miles an hour, and our desire to listen to and watch everyone all at once made that couple of hours surreal. In that brief time we had more change in our lives than we had experienced all year. It really highlighted for us how far removed, in every sense of the word, we had been from the real world.

With barely any room to move we all crowded around the navigation table while Andrew retrieved the 'prezzie box' from his bunk. It was chock-a-block with little parcels from home. Knowing the sense of humour of some of my friends I wondered what I would find. There were teary eyes and much laughter as the contents were shared with everyone. The box revealed lots of cards, letters and photos, exploding party poppers, Year 2000 flutes and new millennium waistcoats, emergency hair removal strips, jelly beans and jam, magazines, books, herbal teas and six pairs of brand new undies. Champagne and chocolates arrived from Andrew (but sadly the ice cream and pizza didn't survive the journey), and buckets of magnificent fresh fruit and vegetables from Don and Margie McIntyre had us smiling from ear to ear. After long months of repetition and rationing the sheer indulgence before us was incredible. It was all just too much for me. I was struggling to keep my emotions under control and I don't really remember eating my dinner that night!

It was our turn to give something so we invited everyone over to Gadget Hut to make New Year phone calls to their families. The excitement was evident and they couldn't wait to get ashore. Most were a bit anxious after all the safety lectures about dangers on the ice, but all were absolutely thrilled to have finally arrived on the continent. That was one of the best bits of the day for me, sharing in the excitement and anticipation of their first steps on Antarctica.

Together we saw the first sunrise of the new century from the historical site of the Australian Antarctic Expedition. It was a magical moment in the most stunning setting on earth. I don't think there was one person there who wasn't indelibly touched by the events of that night.

14.

Home From the Depths

At four o'clock on the afternoon of 8 January Dave appeared at our door and announced that we would be sailing that day. 'The weather's been too good for too long,' he said. 'I know that when it turns it'll be really ugly and I don't want to be here to find out.'

He was right. Ever since the yacht arrived we'd been treated to day after day of the most superb, uncharacteristic weather. Jim and I had never seen anything like it for the whole year. The katabatics still blew regularly late at night and persisted until mid-afternoon, but otherwise it was sunshine and blue skies all around. I think Andrew was disappointed that he hadn't experienced a Cape Denison blizzard during his eight days on the continent, but Dave figured that if we didn't sail soon he might get the opportunity!

Jim and I were ready to go home. Gadget Hut was empty of most of our belongings, the electrical system was decommissioned, repairs and maintenance were done and all emergency supplies had been stored safely in and around the hut. This was it – time to vacate our tiny refuge and sail back into the real world. Surprisingly, I felt little emotion when we placed the final bolt in the front door – no rush of excitement, no sadness, no sentimentality. For me our 'year' had ended the moment the crew arrived on New Year's Eve. Jim and I were no longer alone together and isolated on our piece of Antarctica. Civilisation had begun to catch up with us and I think I was at the 'accepting the inevitable' stage.

The final loading of the yacht and dropping of the mooring lines took ages. I began to feel a great emptiness inside me as I stood watching the final preparations for departure. Was it really twelve months ago that I was in this same spot watching our equipment being unloaded in readiness for our year alone? As I looked around, everything I saw was familiar and loved. I knew every feature of the Cape: the rocky gullies tumbling down from the glacier to the sea, the best views, the curious piles of ancient penguin bones. The historic structures of Mawson's Antarctic expedition were as well known to me as our own Gadget Hut. I knew all the Wedell seals' favourite snoozing spots, all the rocky nests of the skua families, all the caves that the snow petrels had built. Twelve months ago this place had looked big and empty; I'd had a lot to learn. Now it felt as if I was leaving behind not just my footprints but a very important part of my life too. Was I leaving Cape Denison and returning to a life that I might have outgrown? I didn't like the feeling of dwelling in an emotional no-man's-land and was impatient to get on with my life. The waiting around was torturing me.

Spirit motored slowly out of the harbour, leaving a crew of three on shore to stow away the lines in Granholm before returning to the yacht in the dinghy. The narrow channel at the head of Boat Harbour foiled us this time and *Spirit* scraped hard against the rocks on the northern shore. There were a few tense moments as Dave took control and skilfully manoeuvred clear of the potentially serious situation. Was Antarctica taunting us, reminding us that we weren't home safe yet? Once free, and assured that the hull had sustained no damage, we headed out into Commonwealth Bay and waited to haul the inflatable on board, our last task before sailing north.

The sun was shining on the water and it felt as if we were sailing on a blanket of sparkling blue sequins. We motored along at five knots, following the coast at a safe distance but dwarfed by the massive ice cliffs that towered over our mast. Soon *Spirit* was sailing past enormous bergs that had been mere silhouettes in the winter sea ice on our horizon.

I sat alone at the back of the boat and watched my tiny home grow smaller and smaller as the continent drifted peacefully behind us. I could see how the immense size and beauty of the place could create a dangerous sense of wonder, lulling you into forgetting that Antarctica is a cruel, hostile and uniquely remote environment. My respect for the continent was unparalleled, and I had learned how insignificant and vulnerable our existence there had been. When Cape Denison eventually merged with the vast coastline I continued to sit gazing, reluctant to let it go, knowing that I might never see it again.

Life on board fell into the pattern of eating, sleeping and keeping watch. Dave was happy to be safely underway and I think that many of the crew were pleased to be on the homeward leg too. Jim was over the moon and hadn't stopped chatting and smiling from the moment he arrived on board.

Brian took charge of the galley and cooked up a Mexican feast for dinner. It was close to midnight when we ate. Most of us sat out on deck beneath the midnight sun watching the massive bergs glide past as we made our way to the South Magnetic Pole. One particularly unusual berg, with a spectacularly wide band of Peppermint Crisp-coloured ice near the top, caught everyone's attention. Jim photographed and named it 'Lindaberg' after our dear friend Linda, who had been with us in spirit throughout our whole adventure.

The following morning started magnificently. We thought that we were in for a repeat of the day before – calm seas, blue skies and sunshine. It was a bit nippy on deck but on the whole very pleasant. Dave was smiling, everyone was pretty relaxed and it looked as if we were in for a superb day of sailing on the Southern Ocean. We should have known better. In the high latitudes, aptly named the 'screaming sixties', the calm weather can abruptly come to a violent end.

By early afternoon the wind was up and the seas rose. Waves broke over the cabin and everything on deck froze. Conditions continued to deteriorate and the three hours spent outside in the cockpit by those on watch became a trial of endurance. Everyone suffered badly from the intense cold. It was impossible to stay dry and throbbing frozen fingers and toes made keeping watch miserable.

By mid-afternoon things were really rough. A few of the crew were seasick and I even spotted Jim throwing up over the side. I felt okay as long as I could lie flat on my bunk. Actually I spent most of the time lying on the wall rather than the bunk as the yacht heeled so far over with the wind. I couldn't bear to read as it made me queasy watching the words moving about on the page, so I just lay and watched the water wash by the windows. It felt as if we were in a submarine rather than a yacht!

Getting up to walk around was a joke. We were thrown about the cabin, along with everything else that wasn't secured, completely at the mercy of the pitch and roll of the yacht. When vertical, my brain felt as though it was rattling around loose in my head, pounding against the inside of my skull. I found that lying horizontal, with my eyes closed, was the only way I could deal with it.

Not many ate dinner that night. I told Eric that he was a legend for attempting to prepare something anyway. I soon learned that he had a cast-iron gut and always cheerfully took over galley duties when no one else had the stomach to cook, let alone eat anything.

Jim had organised with Dave not to keep regular watch on the return trip to Australia. He wanted the time to relax, thaw out and adjust to the changes we would be going through. Don had sent a crew of ten to pick us up, so Jim felt that he could take it easy without leaving any watch short. He offered to do the graveyard shift each night and relieve one crew member in turn. Everyone would then get an opportunity to catch up on some sleep while Jim took their watch.

But this was not to happen, as it turned out. One member, with minimum sailing experience, was totally overawed by the Southern Ocean. Despite all efforts by the crew to reassure him and assist with his duties, his fears increased to the point where he was incapable of participating in normal yachting life, including keeping watch. He suffered an angina attack three days off the coast of Antarctica and spent the rest of the return voyage confined to his bunk. Jim realised that he had to fill the gap in the watch roster. Three was the minimum required on deck, so he willingly joined Chris and Greg's watch for the rest of the trip.

Every time Jim stepped through the companionway for his three hour stint in the cockpit we were physically separated. After living within two paces of each other for almost the entire year it was unsettling at first to be out of eyesight for so long. During the whole time we lived in Antarctica it was crucial to our safety that we always knew exactly where the other one was. Our separations were brief and timed. In such an extreme climate the dangers were great, so if either of us overextended our time away the other had to assume that something was amiss and gear up to go in search. I found during Jim's watches on *Spirit* that I was always alert for the sound of his voice as he chatted with the guys on deck, and I never relaxed completely until he returned below again.

I felt sorry for everyone when it was their turn to go out and face the wrath of what was building up to be an ugly Antarctic storm. They had to struggle valiantly against the movement of the yacht to get their foul weather gear on before flinging themselves through the companionway door and hooking up to their safety strap. I felt guilty at being snuggled up in my cosy little nest of down, listening to the wind screaming through the rigging and knowing that those on deck were being blasted by driving sleet and snow and dumped by enormous waves.

The bad weather stayed with us for days. It was almost impossible to stand up, let alone walk about, with the boat jolting around so violently all the time. Most off-watch time was spent in the relative safety of a damp bunk. Life below deck was always close and cramped, but during a storm it became very unpleasant. Everyone was cold and damp and suffering from irregular or skipped meals. We had to force ourselves to drink regularly to prevent dehydration headaches from setting in while we rode out the sloppy seas.

On the morning Dave announced that we had crossed the South Magnetic Pole no one whooped with joy or raced around congratulating others. It was simply registered in the log and the replaced watch hit their bunks, eager to get some much needed warmth and shut-eye.

Close monitoring of the barometer showed a steady slide, but we had no appreciation yet of how low it was to go. Talk constantly centred on the grim conditions and the likely effect of the fall in atmospheric pressure. But the sight of three metre high pack ice, tightly compacted and barring our progress north, didn't faze Dave. In his usual manner of dealing with everything as it comes he set a course to cruise up and down in the dreadful swells and poor visibility to look for a break that would allow us a safe passage through. It took two very uncomfortable days of going nowhere to find that break. *Spirit* then delicately made her way through to the open water on the other side and we began our journey north in earnest.

In the bad weather characteristic of this part of the globe a visit to the loo increasingly became a challenge. Once I'd managed to roll out of my bunk and stumble into the head I'd quickly snip the door securely behind me and lean against it while I prepared myself for the next task, which was to get myself into the action position. I discovered that the trick was to work with the movement of the yacht, otherwise it was impossible to hover over the bowl for more than a nano-second before you were shot suddenly forwards or sideways – or, worse than that, the cold porcelain bowl would rise suddenly and sharply to meet you in midair.

As any oceangoing yachtie will tell you, it is important to brace yourself according to the wind and the direction of the sea. I learned that if the wind was coming from the starboard quarter I had to jam my forehead against the wall in front of me, among all the wet foul weather gear hanging there between watches, with my backside pointed at the opposite wall. If the weather came from the port beam I had to lean back and force the back of my head against the wall behind. It was also a good idea to place a foot firmly out in front, ready to stop my body being thrown forward into the wall on the next wave. To make it even more interesting I had to be ready for the times we fell into a trough. This event would cause my legs to suddenly give way beneath me, dumping me unceremoniously onto the seatless toilet bowl or the floor beside it.

Back in my bunk in a horizontal position, with the lee cloth clipped in place to stop me rolling out, I'd lie relieved and pleased with myself. I had accomplished that basic task once more without disgracing myself or adding too many bruises to my current collection. I felt smug that I was getting better at this – and we had been at sea for only three days.

With the screaming sixties living up to their name I began to think that we were never going to escape the high latitudes. On the morning of 13 January the barometer was reading 1005 millibars but by early evening it had dropped to 976. Predictions that we would arrive in Hobart on the 20th were no longer looking good. After several days we were only 290 nautical miles off the Antarctic coast.

Incredibly, the wind hit 63 knots that same day and it was necessary to change from a fully reefed mainsail to the tiny storm jib. Andrew explained to me that having only the storm jib up meant that we could maintain some steering control without being blown around too much. I was all for that as I fought the fear that was threatening to take hold of me. Although I lacked sailing experience it was obvious to me that we were caught in extreme conditions and I felt very vulnerable and at risk. When I saw Dave singing quietly to himself I knew that things were bad!

The waves rolling and cresting all around us were massive. The unpredictable directions from which they approached the boat made the helmsman's job a nightmare. I had read Kay Cottee's story of sailing singlehanded around the world, and the walls of water that she described in the Atlantic Ocean were beyond my comprehension at that time. Well, now I knew what she meant. Suddenly I didn't want to be there any more. It had become another of those times in my life when I wished I could be removed by an angel and transported to some safe (and preferably dry) place.

Tibor, Brian and Eric had not long taken over the watch and were in the cockpit suffering the foul conditions and trying to coax *Spirit* through the maelstrom. They were already soaked and chilled to the bone by the spume and pelting spray in their exposed position on deck. Things were becoming really miserable but they seemed in good spirits and each took their turn at the helm confidently.

The rest of us were lying in our narrow bunks with our arms and legs bracing us against the violent heaving and pitching. Dave was hurled about the cabin as he tried to check that everything was battened down securely. He was just about to empty the pot of cold tomato soup swinging crazily on the galley stove when our whole world quite literally turned upside down.

I remember the fear I'd felt a moment earlier when I heard Brian's loud and urgent warning to everyone on board: 'Hang on!' He'd had no time to do more than call out and then look on in horror at the 25 metre rogue wave bearing down on us. A building 25 metres high has something like eight storeys. *Spirit* mounted the monster beam-on. As we were forced higher up the face the giant wave crested. We had no chance. It knocked us down, pushing us mast first into the deep trough below.

Near freezing water poured into the cabin through the open companionway door. The three men on deck were totally submerged and had to desperately hold their breath. They were all secured to the yacht by their safety lines and whatever they could grab hold of. The mast was pointing down to the bottom of the ocean and the keel was swinging above the waves.

Jim and I were no longer in our bunk but slumped on the skylight hatch of the deckhead. Jim remembers being fascinated by the deep green water he could see below him while he sat looking through what used to be a skylight. I have no memory of anything, so I can only conclude that my head must have connected with something hard and knocked me out.

Brian M., Chris and Andrew were in their bunks when suddenly they were all hurled across the cabin, followed by a barrage of canned food, bedding and equipment stored up forward with them. All knew exactly what had happened and held their breath in anticipation, waiting for *Spirit* to right herself. Alex, who was standing at the chocolate drawer getting her post-watch munchies, was flung against the bulkhead that held all the navigation and weather instruments, and the chocolate drawer went with her. Greg,

Alex G. and Brian managed to stay in their bunks somehow and waited anxiously for the yacht to flip back upright.

Amazingly, *Spirit* righted herself with a mighty sweep and everything and everyone were unceremoniously thrown back again. The team on watch immediately continued to battle the storm as if nothing had happened, and *Spirit* rallied on. There was no time for them to dwell on the drama of the past few minutes – that would have to come later. The instruments, it was soon discovered, were all knocked out and Brian took control, steering by the sheer instinct that comes only from years of sailing experience.

I was dumped in Dave's bunk, a tangle of arms and legs and assorted debris. The large fire extinguisher that had been shaken off the wall bracket nearby followed me in and cut the back of my head open from top to bottom. Tibor, who is a general practitioner, was called off watch to suture the twelve centimetre gash. He jammed me into the bunk to keep me still enough for the job. Alex assisted and Andrew held the torch, pressing Alex against the wall to keep her in place.

With no chance to clip the blood and saltwater-matted hair away from the wound Tibor did the best he could under the circumstances. He had to choose the right moment to plunge each stitch into my scalp because the boat was bucking and lurching unrelentingly. After three strong 'sustaining stitches' he called a halt. It was too difficult to persist and he was worried that he might sew his fingers to my head!

As I lay on my bunk, wet and shivering, trying to stop myself from being thrown around and reopening the wound, the rest of the crew set to work clearing up the mess. Jim told me later that every drawer, locker and storage pocket had disgorged its contents and that they were strewn around the cabin. Salted peanuts were stuck on the ceiling, tomato soup covered the walls and seeped into the refrigerator unit; every nut, bolt and spare part was rolling around on the floor, charts and books were drenched, and items of clothing and bedding were floating here and there.

Everything that Jim and I had on board, including what we wore, was sodden. Even the bunk mattress had soaked up an enormous quantity of icy seawater. Dave lent Jim a set of well-worn thermals from his dirty-laundry bag and gave us a sleeping bag to share. Andrew found me a dry set of clothes and we 'made do' with everything else. Comfort didn't seem to matter too much when our safety was the biggest issue. We were lucky this time – there was no major damage to the structure of the yacht. But could we survive another knock-down?

Dave and Chris took control of the helm for the next six hours. They had no instruments to sail by, just a piece of string tied to a rail to indicate wind direction. They were frozen, exhausted and battling hypothermia as they fought to keep us upright and safe while we rode out the storm. Conditions were definitely on the edge, but I felt surprisingly safe knowing that Dave was in control.

The storm continued. Everyone dealt with the knock-down in his or her own way but all had been either shocked or frightened by our desperate situation. Some were obviously nervous about going back on watch and having to deal with the heaving seas. We came very close to going over again a few more times. It wasn't until the evening of the following day that the extreme conditions eased to 'very bad'. What a relief! It almost felt calm in comparison, but the helmsman still had to be on constant alert for the big ones coming through at very irregular intervals.

Then we saw ice. A large berg, much bigger than *Spirit*, appeared in the distance.

We'd thought we were well past the last of the bergs. In fact Dave had tried to cheer us up earlier by saying how lucky it was that there was no ice around during our tussle with the really big seas. There was no way we could have taken evasive action in such seas and we'd have had no chance if we'd struck a sizeable chunk of ice. It was then that Dave announced that we had survived what was probably the most southerly knock-down in sailing history. I would have preferred no such claim to fame.

Everyone was in amazingly good humour. Some of the conversations were a little strained and the laughter forced as the crew went about fixing and checking every item in the yacht. The final damage tally was reassuring. The dunking had wiped out the weather fax, the generator, the GPS and all other navigational equipment, but most of the gear began spontaneously to work again over the next few days as it dried out.

All things considered, we'd been very lucky to come out of it as lightly as we had. Andrew, who is a motor mechanic by trade, managed to coax life into the generator again later that week. That meant we could flash up the refrigerators before Alex's penguin poo samples completely thawed. The tiny vials of ancient poo were needed for a university project she'd started before sailing south. Returning them to Sydney in the freshest state possible was imperative.

The rest of the trip north to Hobart was rough and uncomfortable. The weather didn't let up much and conditions on board were wearing people down. Alex's description of the trip as 'damp and skankie' seemed to sum it up for us all. The smell of unwashed bodies, damp clothes and bedding made the atmosphere below deck pretty ripe as we pushed our way north. Everyone had stopped daydreaming about fine food, wine and warm weather and begun fantasising about basics such as showers and laundries and dry clothes. Sleep was snatched in short bursts; everyone looked tired and fed up. When Brian M. was caught asleep at the wheel, standing up, in perfect balance with the movement of the boat, we all laughed sympathetically.

On Friday 21 January Dave predicted that we would reach Hobart some time during the night. We were being hit by squalls with winds between 30 and 45 knots, so we were hooning along. The sea temperature was 17°C and the air felt a little warmer. I dispensed with my long underwear for the first time in over a year. My thermal pants felt baggy and breezy and somehow nice against my bare legs.

A cloud of muttonbirds flew over us just as we caught our first glimpse of Bruny Island through the mist off the coast of Tasmania. Our keen senses picked up the earthy smells of the land and Jim and I were overjoyed to see the living coastline with trees and grass, birds and grazing animals. Whereas we had been surrounded all year by a frozen sterile environment, now we were about to be immersed in living, breathing, colourful life. As night descended and we screamed up the Derwent River before a 30 knot wind our eyes were drawn to the twinkling lights that dotted the coast, welcoming us back to civilisation. It all felt so alive.

I couldn't hold back any longer and the tears rolled down my cheeks. I was so happy to be close to home – we had been away such a long time! My thoughts were mainly with Ryan and Ben. I began wondering how they had really felt about our going away for a year. They were always supportive, but did they really miss having us around? I was anxious to see them, talk with them, hold them and know that they were okay. Suddenly someone pushed a mobile phone into my hand and said: 'Got anyone you want to ring?' Within seconds we were talking excitedly to Ryan. It felt incredible that we were on the same planet, let alone chatting with him from only a couple of hundred kilometres away. As we hung up, Jim and I hugged each other. We were going to be seeing everyone after five more sleeps!

Dave's plan was to dock in Hobart, clean up the yacht, do the laundry, stock up with food, refuel, carry out repairs and change over the crew. Andrew, Chris and Dave were staying for the Melbourne leg but everyone else was flying home from Tassie. Marilyn and Julian made up the complement for the trip across Bass Strait. We had to be away again and sailing for the mainland by noon the following day if we wanted to be in Melbourne for Australia Day. The schedule was tight but achievable and everyone was committed to helping us achieve it.

Don and Margie were at the marina waiting to greet us when we pulled in late that night. They had arranged for the customs and quarantine teams to meet us to check passports and permits. As soon as the required formalities were over there were hugs all round as the relief and sheer joy of reaching Australia set in. Margie tempted everyone with a late supper on the deck. The gorgeous aromas of barbecued chicken and freshly baked bread were delightful and my eyes lit up at the sight of a box of scrumptious fruit. Jim and I were then whisked away to the McIntyres' home for a few hours sleep before we set sail again.

Sleep was the last thing we wanted, however. Don and Margie overwhelmed us with their exuberance, their thoughtfulness and their generosity. A feast of berries, cheese, champagne and tubs of rich chocolate ice cream all awaited us. The house smelt deliciously clean and was filled with things we had missed so much – chairs, carpet, taps, hot water, flushing toilets, soft dry beds, colourful ceramic crockery (no plastic), a coffee plunger … I loved the fact that the outside doors could stay open and let the warm fragrant breezes waft in.

I can't even begin to describe how wonderful it felt when Jim and I finally made it to the shower. I just stood under the warm water and cried. Symbolically, to me, that shower meant that we had truly returned to the life we once knew. God, it was great! Margie had stocked the bathroom with beautiful toiletries and after three shampoos and lots of scrubbing, soaping and rinsing we were ready for the ultimate in decadence – the spa! That was when I first saw myself naked in all that time. After 13 months of Antarctic diet and the sedentary life I was amused – well, horrified – at what the wall of mirrors revealed. 'Where did that come from?' I spluttered when I noticed my meaty bottom and rounded tummy.

I borrowed one of Margie's nighties, as my usual night attire of polypropylene long-johns didn't seem appropriate or desirable any more. It was my first feminine item of clothing in a long time and I felt silly in it. I put a polar fleece jacket on over it and joined Jim, Don and Margie, together with Marilyn, Chris and Dave who had come to the house. We sat talking for hours, all the while eating, drinking and gazing around at the wonderful gardens and trappings of civilisation. I didn't want to go to bed in case I woke up in the morning and found it had all disappeared.

That moment for me marked the completion of our great adventure and the fulfilment of my girlhood dream. We relived with Don and Margie the cold and the blizzards, the sunsets and sunrises, the wildlife and the solitude, the glaciers and ice cliffs. We talked about our new appreciation of Douglas Mawson's heroic efforts and, the Antarctic Division's work, and philosophised about polar tourism. We also spoke about the people who'd supported us and encouraged us to follow our dream, along with the thousands of others who had touched our lives momentarily through satellite technology. I wished that my Dad was there to share it with us too, to rejoice in the knowledge that girls really can do things like that.

Climbing into a queen-size bed with smooth sheets and sweet smelling pillows is a joy I'll never take for granted again. Jim and I lay quietly in the McIntyres' guest bedroom, deep in our own thoughts. Sleep eventually came. At one stage I woke up and thought I was still on the yacht and began frantically feeling around for my torch. Eventually I woke Jim and asked if I could borrow his. He reminded me where I was and that I could simply reach over and switch on the light. Fancy that!

It took us another few days to reach home. As we sailed the final leg along the rugged Tasmanian coastline and across Bass Strait, life was one big smile. We negotiated the treacherous Rip with ease and finally sailed up Port Phillip Bay towards Melbourne. We were so close to our home in Flinders that I called out to Jim: 'Breathe deeply, you can smell the home paddock!'

For me there were no whizz-bang feelings, just a deep inner happiness. As the skyline of Melbourne came into view I thought about our amazing experiences of the past year or more. Our personal achievements had been significant and I hoped that we had also inspired others to step out of their comfort zone a little to pursue their own dreams.

Our journey had not been easy – there'd been plenty of trials and challenges along the way. We'd learned to live life at a simpler level but with a far greater intensity. Despite the hardships and difficulties, our bond was stronger for having shared such an extraordinary adventure. 'We must be two of the luckiest people alive,' I whispered to Jim.

He and I are still soulmates, lovers, husband and wife, and best friends, and I couldn't imagine living my dream with anyone else.

Tenzing and the Sherpas of Everest

Judy and Tashi Tenzing

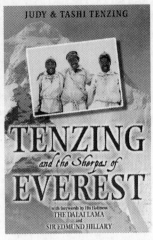

In 2003, the world will celebrate the 50th anniversary of Edmund Hillary and Tenzing Norgay Sherpa's historic ascent of Mount Everest, an event which became a defining moment in twentieth-century adventure and delivered fame and glory to the men who took part in Colonel John Hunt's expedition.

All, perhaps, except Tenzing, who, after a brief honeymoon period with the world's media and political leaders, returned to his humble home in the hill station of Darjeeling, India, and never properly received the credit and plaudits he so richly deserved. In 1986 he passed away, having touched the hearts of all those he came across and having done so much for his people.

Tenzing and the Sherpas of Everest is the inspiring story of this poor and illiterate man who left his small ancestral village in a remote part of the Himalaya and through grit, courage and sheer determination climbed the world's highest mountain and consequently became a hero around the world. But it is also a tribute to Tenzing's family and the Sherpa people who have contributed so much to exploration in the Himalaya over the last hundred years.

Written by Tenzing's mountaineer grandson Tashi and his wife Judy, *Tenzing and the Sherpas of Everest* uncovers one of the great untold stories of world mountaineering and pays long-overdue homage to the Sherpas, without whom the summit of Everest would have remained an impossible dream for climbers the world over.

ISBN 0 7322 6725 0